The

Conversation

The Conversation

Your Guide to Transcendence.

"I will give you a new vantage-point with which to create your memories," he said.

By

Jeff Cannon

W
Walton
Press

Simple Truth LLC
1 Little West 12th Street
New York, NY 10014
(716) 226-8292
info@simple-truth.com

Ordering Information:
Orders by U.S. bookstores and wholesalers please contact the publisher at the address above. Quantity special discounts are available on quantity purchases by corporations, associations, and others. For details, contact the publisher at the address above.

Printed in the United States of America

Publisher's Cataloging-in-Publication data
Cannon, Jeff.
The Conversation : Your Guide to Transcendence / Jeff Cannon

p. cm.
ISBN: 978-0-9908362-0-9

1. Spirituality. 2. Meditation. 3. Self Help 4. Love. 5. Self Realization. 5. Mind and Body. 6. Personal Transformation.
I. Cannon, Jeff. II. Title.
HF0000.A0 A00 2014
299.000 00–dc22 2010999999
First Edition, November 2014
9 8 7 6 5 4 3 2

This book is dedicated to my wife Laura and to our never ending conversations on Love & Perspective.

ACKNOWLEDGEMENTS

I would like to acknowledge all of the teachers who have ever played a part in my own growth and transcendence. They include the people whom I have loved and those who I felt may have wronged me at some time - not realizing that they were some of the most lasting guides I have ever known.

They include the people present on this earth and those who have passed on - yet are with me more now than ever before. They include a rescue cat who turned fear and abuse into love and devotion, as well as a dog rescued from a well that taught me the gratitude of freedom.

They include the grey stone I placed upon a cairn on a beach overlooking the breaking waves of the Pacific, on a trail not far from a mountain top that seemed to overlook the world in all its beauty, on the rocky coast of the Atlantic as the waves thundered off to Europe, on the banks of the Hudson as a hurricane approached and buried beneath the loam as the autumn leaves prepared for winter.

They include the bright colors of a butterfly's wings on a stark winter day, the song of a mourning dove in the morning, and the gentle touch of a lover's hand upon my own.

They include everyone I have ever touched, and those who have touched me in return.

Thank you and Namaste

THE CONVERSATION

"...dwell in shining Ithaca. There is a mountain there, high
Neriton, covered in forests. Many islands lie around it, very
close to each other, Doulichion, Same, and wooded Zacynthos--
but low-lying Ithaca is farthest out to sea, towards the sunset,
and the others are apart, towards the dawn and sun.
It is rough, but it raises good men."

\- Homer, The Odyssey -

What started as a lucid dream of sailing the Aegean grew
into a conversation with what I can only call my higher-self.
That conversation continues to this day in many ways and in
many places since those nights in Ithaca. But Ithaca was where it
began, and much like Odysseus' Odyssey, I have been on a
journey ever since.

My lucid dreams started in an enchanted place - where the
old magic is alive and well, at least for those able to see beyond
the box the modern world has created.

I have known about Ithaca long before my wife and I ever traveled there. What I knew came from history books and one teacher who was fascinated with the seats of human civilization.

On paper the island is named after Ithacis, the son of the sea-god Poseidon. Its first inhabitants arrived close to 3,000 BC or so, and for a while it was the seat of power for the ancient Greek state of Cephalonia.

It is best known as the island Odysseus set sail from in Homer's The Odyssey. It is where Homer established his school around 850 BC. It is also the site of the legendary Cave of the Nymphs.

The year we visited it was a somewhat guarded island. Its year-round residents numbered roughly 3,000, lagging far behind the undocumented population of goats and cats that, by my estimates, easily outnumbered the people.

Nestled in the Ionian archipelago it lies just off the Western coast of Greece. It is just difficult enough to get to that it appeals to those who do not want to be found; which made it perfect for the escape my wife and I had envisioned.

For us, this trip was more than a vacation. It was a celebration for the completion of a friend's forever home. It was the place she planned to retire to after leaving the ateliers of Paris. Designed as a beautiful open air house it was nestled into the Western side of the island's central mountain.

When Corinne first started construction she sent us an open invitation to visit once it was completed. It took several years to finish the house, and this was that year.

The house we arrived upon was elegant and simple. It was painted white and bleached even whiter by the sun and the salt air. The front overlooked the sea between Ithaca and the nearby island of Kefalonia. The back faced the terraced land of thousand-year-old olive trees.

The trees provided shade in the hottest part of the day. Each growing in knotted twists and turns from the rocky soil. Together, they created a scented canopy for anyone lucky enough to nap or daydream in the rustic cots Corinne had set beneath them.

From Corinne's roof-top terrace you could see the white squares that dotted the island's hills of this island and the islands beyond - the homes of neighbors, built of the same clay and whitewashed by the same salt and sun as Corinne's.

Each island was a separate destination, linked only by the white lines of wake that followed the boats that plied the waters between them.

Corinne's home was small but wonderfully built. It had a European vacationers sensibility to it that mixed indoor and outdoor space in a comfortably elegant way.

A wide terrace was both roof and deck, depending on your perspective. The bedrooms opened up to the world outside, where double doors invited the sometimes warm and sometimes cool breeze in.

It was simple and clean lacking any separation with the world outside. The result of a sense of style some people just seem to bring with them no matter where they go.

But perhaps I go too far. Let me stop and breathe, so that I can start at the beginning.

FIRST DAY

Our flight landed in Athens by way of London. We spent a day there before taking took a series of diminishing modes of transportation to Corinne's house. A train took us to the airport. A plane to the island of Kefalonia. A taxi across Kefalonia to the ferry dock, where a ferry took us to Ithaca. It was there that we climbed into a minuscule jeep that I eventually drove the winding toads of Ithaca to Corinne's front door.

Each segment of our journey weaned us further from the world we knew, until we watched the modern world finally slip away from the deck of that ferry.

In the hours that we churned through the Mediterranean, we saw the 21st Century fade as our destination slowly rose from the sea.

At first the earthy greens and browns of Ithaca blended into a blur that contrasted against the blues of the sea and the sky. With each mile the colors sharpened into the olive trees and the grape vines, the earth and the goats that were everywhere.

Ours was a slow and surreal journey that became more distinct as the boat drew closer. The patina that our journey created was from another time.

At some point during that trip we opened an article I had picked up along the way. We learned that the School of Homer had recently been uncovered on the island. We also learned that the Caves of The Nymphs had been identified beneath the broken walls and rubble of earthquakes and human fumbling.

The ruins were all but forgotten until a few years before when a new breed of traveler rediscovered the island, and its secrets were released one by one into the light of day.

After landing on Ithaca, and after the hugs and kisses were over, we clambered into a tiny clap-trap of a jeep and drove along the narrow roads to set our bags inside Corinne's door. No sooner were they down, than we were whisked off to meet a collection of soon-to-be dear friends at a small cafe.

There we were introduced to a revolving group of people from France and Turkey, America and Italy, Germany and points beyond. The introductions were a wonderful tumble of kisses and hugs and heartfelt greetings.

I never really knew just how many there were because there seemed to be a constant flow of people and personalities. Each drifted in and out of the house, the cafes and the beaches that we found ourselves ebb and flow in a modern moveable feast.

The conversation drifted between news and politics, the best beaches and the latest designers. There was no time to unpack or to settle in really. We just enjoyed the good life that we now found ourselves in the middle of.

As afternoon turned to evening, the blur of food and hellos and laughter was the only constant. The heat of the day and blue skies softened into gentle breezes and shades of violet that helped us forget the hot sweaty mess that travel can be. They lulled us into the pace of the island and the easy going flow of food and wine.

The sunset lasted forever. The goat bells rang well past evening and into the night, as if they emanated from deep within the hills themselves. The scent of the sea and the olives filled our noses, and created a path upon which the aromas of the kitchen traveled upon.

Dinner that night was simple. Grilled fish and octopus surrounded by olives and grilled vegetables, all dressed with a drizzle of olive oil and a pinch of sea salt. There was wine and bread and plates that were shared, and yes at the end there was a wonderfully firm Greek yogurt sweetened by honey and the crunch of nuts for dessert.

On the drive home we crept along the narrow roads, watching cats and goats in the headlights before we finally turned into Corinne's home for the night.

It was somewhat late when I turned in. The rest stayed up and caught up as I said my goodnights and wandered off. Wine, mint tea and conversation were the welcoming spirit of the island. They kept everyone else going. But for me, something in my sleep seemed to call me.

I walked down the narrow staircase that clung to the side of the house. Each step was as white as the walls. It was made of the same material as the house, so that each step seemed less a part of the staircase as an out-growth of the house itself. At the bottom the steps became the floor that merged into our room.

At every turn the boundaries seemed blurred. The line between indoors and outdoors had vanished. Our bed opened to the sea and the sky through a pair of large French doors. These invited a gentle breeze in, and freed the mind to wander out. It blew softly day and night, carrying the spirits with it.

The bedding was simple; hand died vintage linen sheets that matched the whiteness of the house itself. They had hung on a line all day and smelled of earth and olives and life.

When I drifted off to sleep, it was to the scents and sounds of the island. The goats and their bells clanked in the distance, stirring my mind to memories of days that I had never seen.

The entire experience was the perfume of Ithaca. It was a perfume of tastes and smells and sounds and textures of a place both foreign and familiar, and this was how my journey began.

FIRST NIGHT

The Ebb and Flow of Existence

That night I dreamed of sailing. I became aware of myself on the deck of a wooden Greek vessel, not from antiquity but still a classic. Beautifully long and sinuous, yet stout and hearty, with a slightly weathered patina to it. It was perhaps thirty feet in length with a black hull and a pair of eyes painted on its prow for luck.

The cockpit that I stood on was open. I had planted my left foot on the floor. My right knee rested on the seat that rose from the hull. At some point in my sleep I had tucked the tiller into the crook of my arm to both steer by and to balance myself with. The wooden tiller disappeared behind me into the wood of the deck and the rudder below.

It was how I always stood when I sailed. It gave me balance and stability. It also reassured me as I held the boat against the push of the winds and the swell of the waves.

It was not a new boat, but it was well taken care of. My eyes noticed the weathered buff beneath the care and experience it held. The tiller was burnished with the oil of many hands before mine. The edges of the wood was worn smooth and round with use. There were slight dents and divots in the flooring where many feet had stood.

I had to wonder how many others had been where I was or had ventured out on her before me. There was something about her that spoke of journeys made well before this one.

The way she moved through the water, the subtle groans of her beams, the way she rode the wind reassured me with a sense of calm that she was stable and secure. I was not worried. I was comforted with her experience. It felt safe to be with her.

As I looked up I noticed the creases in the sails were still being ironed out by the wind. I knew I could not have been sailing for long as there were wrinkles where the sails touched the mast.

I looked to the line where her hull met the water. She was in that moment, rising up and coming to life as she gained speed. She still lacked that lightness that comes with momentum, but as she settled into her place between the water and the air where real boats just skim the waves like porpoises, she felt like home.

We followed the crest of each wave, dipping down the face like a pelican before meeting the back of the next wave and settling into the water with a small shudder. It was like that, a gentle pattern of ebb and flow that never stopped.

Ours was a natural rhythm that all good boats follow. Water and air, surge and pause, tighten and relax.

I looked behind us as the ancient stones of the harbor fell back. A small wake began to bubble from the stern. It disappeared into the waves, severing the last connection I had to the land behind me.

The bells of the goats faded with the shore. The pings and groans of the little craft replaced them as we settled into our new home. There was no doubt my new journey had begun.

I was reminded of what my old Sensei had once said. "You do not need to know where you are going to be on a journey."

Before me the sky was turning dark. There was just enough light to steer by, but not so much as to see the details of the sea around me. My mind stopped trying to navigate by the fading land. I begin to sense our direction by the feel of the wind and the angle of the waves. They were the Yin and Yang between which lay our destination.

A cool breeze had found us. It told me we were outside the protection of the island and in the open sea. The breeze filled the sails into that wonderful curve of white they always seemed to find once they were free.

The main billowed without straining and pulled the tiller gently away from me. It was as if the sails themselves were lifting us further from the safety of the harbor.

That was the moment I first noticed him. He may have been there before. I have no way of knowing. He sat as if he had always been there. A watery wetness defined him. It defied solid borders. He was more elemental than human. Almost as if a part of the ocean had shaped itself to keep me company.

I call him *he*, not because he was a man, but because there was a masculinity about him. It was as if his energy mirrored my own and made me think of him as a *he* rather than a she or an it.

In all honesty, he was not really anything. He simply was. As with so many things that cause our brains to fill in the gaps of life on its own, he caused mine to fit the ambiguity of his existence into a form it was comfortable with.

The problem was it couldn't. I have learned that our brain doesn't always get it right. This time it stopped trying at a certain point. Instead of forcing him into a form, my brain simply accepted what he was not, and then let it go.

When he spoke, it was more than words that reached me. His voice was larger than letters and longer than sentences. It reverberated with emotion and context. It was layered with scents and memories and entire experiences. There was a deeper, richer understanding to what would be our conversation.

It was as if the intent of his thoughts reached out to envelop both of us with all the rich history and meaning that words alone can never convey.

The word transference is more of what this seemed to be. I had to let go of the concepts my brain tried to find comfort in. I had to push past my own ego, telling me what was and was not possible. In many ways that is what the realm of dreams is for. To transcend logic so that we can truly experience what is.

My brain struggled to understand the enormity of him. The lack of defined boundaries, the voice beyond speech. Both were hard to grasp. It was as if my brain was trying to fit him into a preconceived idea of what a being can or cannot be. It was an exercise I had to force myself to let go of.

I never really solved the riddle of what he was. I just accepted him and continued on. In one sense I was sailing. In another it was completely different. We flowed, we drifted, we were in motion but not in a linear sense. Our movement was not defined by the boundaries of the horizon, but by my own notions of where we were, and even then I couldn't swear to it.

He seemed to understand my thoughts before I spoke them. As if he was connected to the individual neurons of my brain, he picked up on my thoughts almost before I could.

Ours was less a verbal conversation than an exchange of understandings. It was layered with intent and emotion and memories I had forgotten I even had. There was greater depth and meaning than we have ever achieved through the spoken word alone. My thoughts were free from the filters that normally limit us; free from the distractions we try so hard to speak around.

I feel it necessary to make a note here. In reading through my manuscript the quotation marks I used fail to convey all that actually passed between us.

Just as my brain struggled to define him in our first moment, I still struggle to define my experience through the written page. It is something that simply cannot be done - perhaps it is the equivalent of reducing a twelve-dimensioned experience onto the flatness of a two-dimensional piece of paper.

The quotes I settled on connote the direction of our conversation even though they fail to bring the full richness and meaning to life.

In the end, I sacrificed the depth of our experience in order to communicate the broader message as best I could.

I encourage you to read between the lines and to add your own subtext. I doubt you will do much harm to the lessons that transpired.

I could feel the changes in the waves and the wind as my friend, the boat and I distanced ourselves from Ithaca. We had, in many ways, become one.

The waves smoothed out from the rough chop of the shore to the easy swells of deep water. The gusts breathed together into a strong steady breeze. They gave us the curious sense that we were settling into a long journey that would last longer than just this one night.

Minutes, hours, seconds? I don't know how much time passed, but the dark shadows of the island were gone. They blended into the waves around us. There was no longer a boundary between land and sea. There was only darkness and an area above it filled with stars.

Above those brilliant points of lights shone bright. Below the waves flowed out and into a void. Together they gently picked us up and set us back down in their easy rhythm, returning the hull into the soft cradle of water we rode on.

This lull gave me a moment to take stock of where I was. Traditional oars rested in their brackets on either side of the cockpit. Above them, the wooden hoops of the sail pulled against the mast. The pressure of wind and water balanced and stiffened the boat, making it stronger than it could have ever been on land.

The sliding door to the cabin was firmly closed against the deck, sealing whatever lay below in what I hoped was an airtight hull.

I smiled to myself and to my little crew as I relaxed into the lucidity of my dream. I did not know exactly where I was or where I was going, but I was okay. I sat down with the tiller still tucked into the pit of my arm knowing it was all good and safe and solid.

She was a traditional craft able to weather most storms. Across from me, my companion seemed able enough. Not quite a seaman, but quiet, and I would take quiet over someone who knew every inch of a boat by name on most voyages any time.

My body hardly moved as we swayed with the waves. His flowed gently back and forth in time with the tiller. I realized the boat did not need me. She guided herself, balancing between my needs and those of the dream I was in. Balancing on the horizon, the sky above, the water below, and the wind in between.

I reminded myself from time to time that my here and now was a dream and that I needed no plans other than to follow the heartbeat of the sea. My only goal was to soar on the water like a porpoise or a gull on the air just above it. There were no charts before me, and the binnacle remained closed as we moved to our destination in the inky darkness of the night and the sea.

I smiled at my guest at one point. I was still unsure how he had gotten on the boat. But I knew he belonged just as I did. He simply sat there, at the forward edge of the cockpit. His long limbs thin and angular, wrapped around themselves, hugging his form to the deck. He seemed to sway with the waves as I began to. It was as if our bodies moved in unison with the waves that flowed below us.

The darkness kept me from seeing his features clearly. He was painted with the color of the sea and sky, blending into both and standing out against the wood of the boat. One moment he was soft and vague, the next he was defined by details.

Even if there had been light I'm not sure how clear he would have been. His physical form was in a constant state of motion even when he was still. There was enough to him to know he was there, but not so much to create a distinct memory.

He was more of a presence than a body, more of an impression than a well-defined figure. He existed without taking up space, and I was fine with that.

At some point I remember seeing stars twinkle through him, or perhaps from within him. I decided he was solid; in the same way the surface of the ocean becomes solid when it rolls up onto the beach. At that moment it is firm and distinct as it takes on the shape of the sand only to roll back and once again become fluid.

We sat there for the longest time. He, a wiry bundle of energy that moved even when he stayed still. Me, a physical block that remained motionless even when I swayed with the sea. It was as if he did not want to disturb the air around him, and I could not help but do just that.

For the first few minutes we just looked at each other. He observed me and I him. My thoughts were intent on steering a boat that seemed to steer itself. His thoughts calmly observing me and taking it all in.

It was I who reached out first. Not with words but with the thought of how best to say hello. What came out was a simple question that tried to define the new sounds I found inside me.

He welcomed my question with a smile.

"Do I know you?" I asked.

He smiled again. He seemed to say we had known each other for all time.

"But, who are you?" I asked.

His smile cut the silence again as the essence of his words rang through.

"Energy."

I could feel my eyebrows knot and my eyes squint as I tried to comprehend the volumes his one word contained.

"Energy?"

The question emerged without my lips ever moving.

"I am the same as you. I am energy. Only my energy is unencumbered by humanity."

It was not said with pride. It was said as the simple fact that it was.

"Where did you come from?"

He didn't smile exactly. His answer smiled from within him.

"I have always been here. I always will be here. I am no different than you. I am from within you and from without."

"That doesn't make any sense."

"Think beyond the physical. Beyond your own limitations," he said. "Give yourself permission to accept what is possible and it will be possible."

I was swimming in words and thoughts and ideas as I tried to makes sense of what was occurring. It was a dream, but not.

After a moment's pause he continued, "You create the world you live in. That world is simply a mirror of your energy. The energy you put out is the energy you receive. It is why the physical world you live in is so limited. It is the world you allow yourself to be a part of. That is why I am from within you. It is why I am a part of you while still being from without."

I let go of my ego. I let go of my judgment. It was a dream but even in this dream I needed to have my feet on solid ground. I allowed myself to accept what he said and to float in it even if it lasted just for a moment.

"You only see what you allow yourself to see. You are a part of the world you created for yourself at every level. If you are happy or sad the world around you shifts to meet the energy of your mood.

"It may change only slightly. But it changes nonetheless. You see the skies a shade lighter or a shade darker. The air expands or contracts. It may not be visible to your eye, but you know it when it happens."

And I did know. I had witnessed it myself, in youth, in adolescence, as an adult.

"But how did you get here?" I asked.

"There was an energy." was all he said.

"I don't understand. We're miles away from anywhere."

"A mile is but an inch if you step back far enough. No matter where you go the energy of you is always there. In truth, we are all just moments away from wherever we are going. The true distance is in knowing why we are going there."

Each word went through me and past me, leaving the impression of their greater meaning.

"You think in terms of distance and time," he said. "Those are constructs to make you more comfortable while in the human experience. They are mere coordinates for the moments in your life."

He understood my thoughts before I did.

"When you learn to think in terms of impressions and energies you will begin to understand to navigate existence.

"The impressions you carry with you are what contain the energy of existence. That energy is what your memories are made of. Your memories are not the location or the time of your life, but the energy that makes it real for you.

"The thoughts of Love or the absence of Love carry far more import than longitude and latitude, minutes and miles."

At that moment I couldn't help but think of my travels that day. At times I stared at the fabric of the seat in front of me for what seemed like hours, separated by moments of focus as I ate my meal or read my book.

Even while reading there were moments of hyper-focus where I was a part of the words on the pages. There were also moments of emptiness where it seemed like entire chapters passed by where nothing stuck.

"Then why are you here?" I asked.

"I am here to give you a new vantage point from which to view existence, a new perspective."

He paused as I let his words sink in. I was still unsure of what was going on but I didn't want to wake up without finding out.

"Each one of us experiences the events of our existence from a unique perspective. Your perspective is different from that of anyone else. No matter how slight the difference, each of our experiences differ. It is the details that make all the difference in the universe. Understanding your perspective is the first step to understanding what is reality and what is *your* reality.

"You experience life from many states of consciousness and many levels of awareness. The world around you fades in and out of focus depending on where you place your attention. Your consciousness does the same for all eternity. Your experiences grow and fade as your focus shifts through life. It is your own awareness, not the events in your life, that is important.

"Some moments gain in importance and others fade depending on how much energy you apply to each memory. That is what defines how much each becomes a part of your life.

Your desire for a particular life creates that life for you based on the experiences you allow in. Just remember, your life is different than your existence. Your life is temporary. Your existence is not."

I allowed my mind to wander through what he had said. It came back with an image that looked like it was on the page of a presentation. A circle called *life* nestled within an enormous ellipse labeled *existence*. I was embarrassed by the imagery, but it gave me the grounding that I so needed.

"The energy you put out is the energy you receive. Fear, anger, Love, desire – each of these emotions shades your experience more than the sights and sounds and actions ever could. Those feelings are more real than whatever it is you think you see or hear or taste.

"You choose to live how you are living. How you experience life and how you remember it is based on the energy you place on every event you live through. That is what forms your existence. It is why some people live a lifetime in a single breath and why others spend an eternity breathing without ever experiencing what life truly is."

"I understand what you are trying to say, but there is a point where a single breath and an entire lifetime cannot be compared."

I said, or thought really.

"Take time out of the equation," was all he said. "Time is a marker for your memories and nothing more. It is no different than longitude and latitude, but it is not your experience.

"The human experience you are traveling through depends less on how long you live and more on how deep each of your experiences run. The understanding you gain in life is based less on what you take from life and more on what you give in life.

"Your greatest moments of despair and joy are the most tangible of experiences. They stay with you for an eternity.

"The moments that are quickly forgotten are those points of existence where little energy is sent or received. It is up to you to decide which of the moments in your life are to be kept and which are to be left to float by without reflection.

"When you read a book there are moments when you cannot remember what you just read. There are moments when you travel that you pass by miles and miles of scenery, yet you cannot remember what the view looked like, or what you were thinking, or even what you were doing.

"Where were you during those moments? Your body was there, but you most certainly were not. You left with no experience of what transpired. You have no memories because you expended no energy on what was."

"Am I here right now?" I asked.

"Your body may not be here right now, but you most certainly are. You are here because your consciousness is here."

"So my consciousness is what is real."

"Your consciousness is your everything. It is your entire being. Your awareness is that point of connection between your consciousness and all of existence. It is your conduit into all that is. It is why a dream can be more real than any waking moment.

"Forget the physical. That is temporary. Your true existence is the energy behind it. Everything else you know is a reflection of that energy. Your thoughts, your actions, your being are a mirror of the consciousness that reflects the energy that is all around.

"There are many points in time in which you can be awake, without awareness. It is during those moments that you may be conscious but without awareness. You exist, but you are not aware of the world around you. It is like reading a book, not being aware of the words on the page you have read. It is like walking down the street without being aware of the people you just passed.

"At those times there is no trace that you were even in that moment. You fed so little energy into your experience that your existence made no memorable impression, not just in the physical world, but in all of existence.

"This is why you are here. Your consciousness has woken. It has placed your awareness fully on this moment. You are aware of your existence not because of your body, but because of your consciousness."

"Where did you come from?"

"I came together from everywhere and nowhere. I exist in a different way than you do. Without the shell of humanity I am not held by time and place. Those words mean less than you can imagine. Existence is not about when and where. It is about thoughts and ideas. It is about energy.

"In time you will understand. Until then just know that you are everywhere because you are connected to everybody and everything. Even if that connection is but a thread, it still exists."

He smiled in that non-smile way. It was a feeling that I would grow to appreciate. "For now, I simply am," he said.

We sat for a bit in silence as I gradually allowed myself to let go of my need for a solid foundation solid ground and accepted his words.

I could feel his energy as he began again.

"For now, just know that everything in existence is in constant motion. Like the sea, everything is in a constant state of flow and of change. On the surface, when two planes meet, there is turbulence. Beneath, it is calm. The further from the surface you travel, the calmer it becomes.

"It is like that in life. The stillness you seek is not found on the surface but deep within you. It is a state of mind, not being."

"Is that why you appear misty to me? Out of focus?" I asked.

"It is. We exist on two different planes. Where we meet our individual planes touch and create the turbulence you see. You carry your humanity with you. I no longer need the shell of humanity to exist. I do not need the ground or the sky to be. I have found my place. I simply am.

"You will find yours soon enough. You have already found yours in some ways. You will see that in truth there is no form. At the core of everything there is simply energy. Your reality is based on how you perceive the energy that is. All that you know is a reflection of the energy that is you.

"The atoms that create your physicality are nothing compared to the space that is between them. What you recognize as real is in truth the energy that is found between the atoms holding them together.

That energy is what your consciousness is aware of. That is why your perception influences the world around you. That is why you create the world around you. Your energy fills the gaps between the atoms to create existence. It is the energy that holds your world together. That energy is your reality.

"Just like you?"

"Very much like me."

"Then why are you here? Why now?"

"There is energy."

"There is energy?"

"You are alive with energy. You are at a crossroads between two planes. There is turbulence. It is your time to talk."

I shied from the offer. "What about?" I said.

He smiled, knowing, not pressing.

"Tides and waves. The ebb and flow of life. The cycles and stages that are the nature of existence. You have experienced much. There is much turbulence beneath your surface that seeks calm. With understanding you can step through the surf and into the sea where you will find the balance and calm you seek."

31

I did not argue. Instead I settled back into those words and into the deck. I found myself in a calm I had not known. It was quiet as we allowed the motion of the waves to speak for us.

"Look around," he said. "What do you see?"'

"The ocean."

"Is that all?"

"I see stars, waves, shades of blue and black."

"You don't see anything else?"

It was less a question. It was an invitation for me to answer.

"From above the ocean looks flat and dark," he continued. "But from down here it is alive. It is an undulating carpet of waves and curves, of energy and endless motion.

"Life is not about what you see. It is the perspective that you see it from. At the center of everything is a single event, a single point of energy. That event sends ripples out. Those ripples become waves. It is the waves that you experience, not the event itself. It is why we can see the same event and have a different description of what occurred.

"Everything you see is an echo of the original. How you perceive an event is based on your perspective and where you are when you experience the waves of energy as they reach you.

"Your being has less to do with what occurred than with the vantage point from which you experienced it.

"How you experience existence depends on how you perceive the energy of existence and its echo. That is why in the end there is little you can do about the events in your life, but there is much you can do with how you respond."

There was silence in my dream. Beneath that silence there was the sound of the wind and the waves. It was the quiet calm within me that I heard. It was as if you could hear the bubbles in the froth bursting as they sailed from each wavelet. Each one distinct from the roar of the ocean.

"Are you happy or sad?" he asked.

"Are you positive or negative?" he continued.

"Are you open or closed?" he smiled.

"Each of these matter far more than whether a wave is about to crest or is about to roll beneath you and past your boat. Like all things in existence waves never really begin or end.

"At some point a wave may they roll into your consciousness. That is the moment they become real for you. That is the moment everything becomes real for you. The moment a wave of energy enters your consciousness it becomes a part of your existence. It is now an event for you.

"The second you expend energy on something, it is real. How real something is depends on the energy you feed it. Some events become so real they become part of tomorrow's memories. Others are forgotten before they even arrive. Through it all existence continues to pass around you and through you in an endless stream of energy.

"The universe is no different. The moments that you remember most vividly stay with you because of the energy you gave them. How that energy wraps around you and becomes a part of you depends upon your perspective.

"The flash of a second and the toll of an hour matter less than the vantage point from which you experience them. It is your vantage point that creates memories that last forever or that quickly fade. Each is brought to life through your energy."

The boat shuddered briefly as the waves rebounded off the hull. Each pushed us forward to whatever destination we were heading. Each balanced us against the forces of the wind and the weight we carried. The energy that remained moved us forward.

It seemed as if we were in the middle of a game as the cosmic forces fought over our speed and direction. Much like the calm in the eye of a hurricane, there was a wall of chaos spinning around us. But in the middle of it all we were simply able to be.

"With all of the forces bouncing back and forth, how do you know what actually happens," I asked?

"What actually happens matters less than how you experience it. How your experience it is how you will remember it. In memories there is energy. In energy there is existence.

"The truth of an event is transformed the instant it occurs. They are transformed based on the energy of those witnessing it. Not just when those events occur but for the rest of existence.

"At times it may seem like the present is the most important part of being. On some levels it is. On others how you interact with the energy of a moment is far more important than how you lived in that moment.

"The energy you create in the present can start a wave that wave will be with you for the rest of your life. It will change depending on how you live your life. This is how a bad memory becomes a good lesson. It is how a good memory can trap you in a bad cycle that can last forever.

"Once you become comfortable with the way a memory is remembered, is the moment you lose yourself to that memory. When realize that your life is but an event in the entirety of your existence, is the moment you are able to free yourself."

"How will I remember this moment?" I seemed to ask.

"Like every moment, this moment is but an event within an event. You may not remember it, but it will still be a part of you for all eternity. On one level this moment will be gone before you are even aware of it. On another this moment will shape your future and the perspective with which you see everything from this moment forward.

"Your body does not always work fast enough to catalogue every moment for you. To your brain some events will be but the blink of an eye, but it will stay with you forever. It will exist in the stirring of an idea. It will appear as a notion that you will smile upon and then forget. It is nothing, but it is everything. All moments in life can be like this.

"You experience the events of your life based on your perspective, not on the actuality of an event. How your life is lived and enjoyed depends on your vantage point, not on the outcome of an event that once seemed so important."

I looked out at the water and the sky. The long, slow motion of the boat, interrupted by the occasional shudders of a wave, set my mind following his path as if it were a meditation.

"How do you find that perspective?" I asked.

"You find that perspective by turning your awareness and seeing the world from a different angle," he said.

"You question. You explore. You remind yourself to remain comfortable with the fact that existence is never stable. It will forever change. As will you.

"Your perspective grows as you learn to know yourself. It evolves as you realize where you are in your existence. Once you understand where you are you become aware that all of your experiences are relative to your energy. Time is relative. Place is relative. So too is the world as you understand it to be.

"Your senses create a lens through which you see your world. That perspective guides, and is guided by, your idea of existence. It is part of the human experience you are a part of. You see your world through your emotions, as your mind enables you to see it.

"Your perspective changes when you are angry or when you are happy. You experience the world differently through the filters of your emotions and your energy. Anger and happiness, loneliness and Love, all filter the energy that comes to you."

He paused for what bordered on an uncomfortable moment before he started again. I was on the verge of my thoughts gelling together when his interrupted my own.

"Look around you. What do you see?"

I told him what I saw. "I still see water and stars, waves and the boat. I see you."

"Before you ask a question about life, first look around yourself; search for the patterns of existence. They do not change. Your answers will be found in nature.

"When you look at the sea from the window of a plane what do you see?"

I shrugged in thought if not in actuality. "I see a flat carpet of greenish blue?" I said.

"There are no waves to be seen from that height are there?" He asked. "There are no contours."

"Yet from down here you do not see the entire ocean, instead you see each wave as it rolls past. You see each wave as it builds, crests, and dissolves back into the sea.

"It is no different from any point in existence. From space, your world seems like a non-moving marble of bluish-green. Yet when you see the world up close you learn the nuances and the details that eluded you from space.

The same is true for people and for emotions. When you first meet somebody you see their general features. As you come to understand them, you learn about their nuances and their emotions. You learn about their desires and their needs. You begin to see the details of who they are. From either vantage point they still act in a way that is consistent with the nature of all things.

"When you look at the water from a closer vantage point you see that upon each wave there are wavelets. You see that each wavelet is pushed one way or another by the wind or by the action of the currents beneath the surface.

"Each wavelet may seem unpredictable. They are not. The actions of each wavelet is quite consistent with the unseen forces that act upon it. To know how the unseen wind and currents change that wavelet you must dive in and see the nature of those forces. Once seen, you will understand.

"If you dive down and follow your thoughts, you will see the waves from below. How you react becomes predictable and consistent with your perception of the world you live in.

"As the light filters through the waves it refracts off of the water's surface. You begin to feel the forces beneath the waves.

The push and pull of the currents move the entire ocean this way and that. Those same forces also move you. You feel the waves themselves. You are moved by them. You become a part of them. You learn to flow with the energy that is created as they circulate the oceans around the planet.

"This is no different than with any other energy. Whether you are in or out of the human form, the more vantage points you see from, the more perspectives you have and the more you are able to learn. When you truly see the energy of existence you see the forces that shape existence and you see clearly.

"The more you learn about a person, the more you understand who they are. When you learn about the pain and the Love that have moved them, you learn about the energy they carry and that has formed them into the person they are. You understand what has created the life they now inhabit. When you see their past, you begin to see the path that lies ahead of them. You become enlightened to them and by them.

"In all of this, nothing has changed except your perspective. Each nuance is like the force that creates a wavelet on the ocean. It could be as powerful as the wind or as seemingly small as a pebble dropped into the water miles away. Each exerts energy. Each is another circle of life to be experienced."

41

It was at once so simple, yet so entwined, once you saw beneath the surface.

"How can we compare a wavelet to a life?"

"Neither is real. Each is a reflection of the energy that began as a ripple. Each is a link in a circle that connects us all in the web of existence.

"Every event that someone experiences is a part of that circle. It is a circle of energy that evolves and grows in size. Just as wavelets ride upon a wave, every wave rides on the endless tide of the ocean. Those tides in turn ride on the energy of the earth. The earth rides upon the energy of the sun. The sun upon the spiral of the universe. "There is an ebb and flow to each of these cycles, yet each behaves in the same way. They are echoes of the others.

"Being conscious of the cycles of existence and being aware of how they affect you is a lesson learned when you are able to view your own life from a new perspective. Each provides insight into the forces of existence, and yes, that includes your own reactions to what is.

"What you see of the ocean depends on your vantage point. The ocean does not change. Your perspective does.

"How you view yourself and how you view others depends less on who they are and more on your perspective. How close you are to your subject effects your experience. Where you stand in their circle transforms your understanding of them. Each is the sum of everything that has ever happened to them and to you.

"You think in terms of linear space and time. That is a very flat perspective to exist in. That only provides you with a single perspective when there are three-hundred and sixty degrees to a full circle.

"Your view of the world is limited by your past experiences. Those experiences shape your current awareness and your view of the future. When you are aware of the web of energy that connects everyone and everything you become aware of your actions and those of all that is around you.

You become aware of the ripples that a pebble creates and how those ripples can change the outline of continents. It never stops. It continues in all directions, just as a wavelet effects and is affected by the wave it rides upon. You effect and are affected by the world you bring with you.

"What you experience in life is wholly dependent on the vantage point from which you witness life. There is a never-ending flow of cycles and circles that influence and are influenced by your own energy. Just like the waves in the ocean. Just like the galaxies in the cosmos. Each continues on its course in a never ending ebb and flow of energy that responds to the forces it encounters. It never stops, it rebounds from each and carries on its path forever changed, but unable to stop.

"If you doubt this, simply step back and observe. When you step back far enough, you see that galaxies spiral in great cosmic circles, planets revolve around the sun in giant ellipses. Moons revolve around their planets, and even planets spin around their axis.

"Ocean currents, weather patterns, seasons, day and night, they all move in circles. Even the concept of life and death form an incomprehensibly large circle. If you are to make sense of it you simply have to step back to see it fully.

"One person may see life as a flat line that ends in death. That is what you see if you look at life from a physical perspective. But if you step back and see the spiritual existence life becomes but an arc on the much larger wheel of existence. In that moment you will realize that life takes up less than a tick on the face of the clock of eternity.

"Just realize that there are no flat lines anywhere. If everything is a circle, why limit your thinking to a linear view of space and time? A flat line only exists when you are too close to see the larger arc that we are all a part of."

I remember feeling uncertain with where to go. No matter how lucid, I knew this was a dream. I also knew that there was something very un-dreamlike about it. I was not directing. I was observing on so many levels.

He seemed to pick up on the direction of my thoughts when he spoke.

"In many ways we are like a trout in a stream. We are all observers. We observe the energy that is existence as it flows past us. We acknowledge the opportunities for balance. We even try to connect to that balance before it passes by, we simply do not always catch that opportunity before it is gone.

"All around us is a sea of energy. We observe the ebb and flow of that energy through the filters we have chosen. Ours is a shared reality. It is different for each of us because we witness it through the lenses of our own experiences.

"When there is an event in the infinite sea of existence, you sense its wave as it passes. For most events that wave is small and subtle. It washes past gently pushing and pulling your own energy this way or that. At other times the event is simply too great for your consciousness to comprehend. In those times the shell of humanity protects your consciousness so that you can experience that wave without being drowned. It is the human experience that allows you to observe and learn and grow, free from harm.

"You and I are in the same ocean. We witness the same events. We simply do so from different vantage points. Our perspectives enable us to see the same occurrence through different lenses.

"We will both learn and grow from each event as it passes. Because we witness it from different vantage points we will both feel the impact differently. Those vantage points are created by our individual histories and experiences.

"In the human experience that you call life, yours is a single vantage point from which to witness the energy of existence. Yours is a limited experience from which your consciousness will eventually grow and evolve beyond.

"Beyond the safety of your human shell exists your consciousness. It lies is a sea of pure energy called Love. That energy never stops flowing, never stops moving. Just as every desert is filled with grains of sand, every ocean is filled with drops of water, the endless sea of existence is filled with individual points of consciousness that are our true selves. You and I both exist in the same moment of eternity and in the same sea of energy. We simply experience it from different vantage points. From our own points of consciousness.

"The forms we both fill are but mirror images of our true selves. They are our own simple truths. It is why you so often feel that you are observing your life from the outside, because in truth you are."

His words focused my thoughts. I could see the grain of the wood that was the deck. It was outlined against the expanse of ocean beyond. Both were in view, but while the deck was in sharp focus the waves quickly blurred into the distance. One detailed, the other endless.

"If we both see reality differently, where is the truth?"

"The truth is you," he answered. "Every occurrence that you and I share is an echo of its true nature. What we experience is a ripple within the purest energy of existence.

"While you may feel as if you float in and out of consciousness every day of your life, your true self remains. It is here that existence is bound together by the energy that flows through all of us.

"That energy connects us, includes us, nurtures us and in turn draws from us. We exist in a never ending current of energy that flows just as the currents in the sea flows through the water that carries them.

"When there is an event in the energy that binds us all together we each feel its ripples in our own way. How we feel that energy depends on the energy we surround ourselves with. Together those create our perspective and provide the vantage point from which to view the reality of existence.

"The energy that binds you to every event you have ever experienced both creates your consciousness and is created by it. It weaves itself through your path and flows to create the collective consciousness we all exist in.

"You experience the energy of existence on one plane and I on another. Neither is better or worse. They are simply different vantage points with which to experience the never-ending flow of Love within which floats each of our existence. It is why everything changes, because nothing is solid."

It was moments like this in my dream where I wasn't sure if I was dreaming at all. The voice was so clear and vivid. My thoughts were so basic and elemental that it was as if I were awake and experiencing our conversation as awake.

There were no ripples in time or folds in reality to make me think otherwise. Here I was, on a boat, in a sea, sailing to nowhere and completely content with it.

"Then all of this?" I waved my arms, "our entire existence, is just energy?" I asked.

"It is. Energy is the medium. You are existence. Just like the sea, energy holds eternity together. It is in that energy that the ripples of our experiences ride. There is no time. There is no separation of past memory from present consciousness. There simply is.

"You may place our awareness in any direction, that is where your consciousness exists. Not because of where you are or what you are doing, but because you are aware. Time is not the continuum, you are.

"The strength of your continuum depends on the depth of your consciousness. The depth of your consciousness depends on where you have placed your awareness, how present you are. You exist because you have focused your awareness on a single point of your existence.

"When you become angry or excited you create an event with your energy. When you Love a piece of art, a person or a flower you create an event. It is the focus of your own energy that creates an event in the sea of existence. A ripple emanates from your consciousness that ripples outward and touches everything, you do.

"The more energy you place upon an idea or an emotion, the greater is your impact. The greater your impact, the greater the influence you have on the collective energy we all exist in. Your energy creates an impression, not just in the here and now but for all time and space. That impression is your wave. Do you now see how your wave can transform oceans?

"Present, past, future, those are just boundaries that you created while passing through the human experience. In truth there is no time. Time is nothing more than a marker for where you are. It is no different than longitude and latitude. It is nothing more than a plane that helps you conceptualize life in a way that you are comfortable.

"The human experience you are passing through is like a gentle rain on a pond. Each raindrop makes an impact as it lands on the pond's surface. That raindrop creates a ripple when it strikes. Each splash lasts for but a moment but it is the ripples that last.

"In time the drop is gone, but its energy remains. It has added to the pond. Even though its effect may be imperceptible it has changed everything, forever. The pond has become a little fuller. The water has become a little cleaner.

"There is a new energy that each ripple carries with it. It may be unnoticeable on the surface. Yet beneath the surface that drop has made a difference throughout the pond as its ripples echo back and forth.

"Your existence witnesses the raindrop and everything connected to it. The energy of your existence makes an impact on the Universe and all of existence every moment of your life.

"Your energy effects everything long after you have left the shell of humanity behind. You will be remembered long after your body fades away.

51

That memory is your energy and your ripple. That is the impact you have on everything. Your energy will forever affect others in ways you cannot even begin to imagine.

"Once you think or dream or act, no matter how large or small, your energy has changed the universe and all of existence. The greater your energy, the larger your ripples and the greater your impact. Whether you improve the pond or prevent it from coming together depends on the quality of your thoughts, your actions and your energy. Each raindrop may not seem like it makes an impact, but it does. The better your energy, the purer is the water that flows into the sea."

Conceptually I knew that everything he was saying was true. It was echoed in the evolving contemplation of physicists and philosophers throughout time. But still I felt the tiller in my hand, I felt the deck beneath my feet. I reached over to feel the cool water of the sea. He smiled, knowing what I was doing.

"Think of everything that is around you," he said. "It is real because you have said it is real. Physically the reflection of the water is simply the energy of the setting sun that you have taken in through your eyes. To you though, it is more. It is all the sunsets you have ever seen. All those memories you stored of water and reflections and sunsets from the past and those you imagined to see, that are yet to be, are simply energy.

The fragrance of jasmine that enters your nose calls upon the memory of a garden that you have held onto from childhood. The energy of food is what stirs your mouth to water. It may make your heart yearn for a memory of a lover, yet that energy is more real than the physical sights and sounds before you.

"In that moment the energy of your memory has more effect on you than the energy of what you call reality just inches away. Whether imagined from the past or experienced for the first time, your brain translates the energy that your senses and mind come contact with into an electrical impulse. Your brain brings that impulse to life and that energy, no matter where or when it is from, is now a part of your experience, a part of your life.

"Your brain only sees the physical, because your brain is there for your survival. Your mind, however, does not differentiate. It combines all your energy into an experience.

"That is how the image of a rose, the smell of a wet rain, or the taste of a sweet berry becomes more than just the physical experience. It is why it matters less that it is an actual rose or the dream of a rose from years past. If it is the actual smell of rain or the scent of a candle that stirs your senses to life, it does not matter. Each can be just as real as the other, because each carries the energy that expand out to form your reality."

"But flavors and scents fade with time."

"They only fade if you allow them to fade. The Love you feel for someone will build and deepen if you keep it alive. That same Love will also fade into nothing if it is left alone.

"Have you ever wondered why you salivate at the smell of food? It is not just the food itself, but the memories of meals past that stir your taste buds to life. The anticipation you have of the food to come is the culmination of the smells in the present moment as well as the energy from all the experiences you have ever had with the food you are about to partake in.

"It is why your heart can cry out for someone who you have not seen in years. They may no longer be the same person. But it is not the person that you miss. It is the memories. It is the energy they have left behind.

"All of those memories may not be real in you're here and now, in the physical sense. Yet they are very real in their ability to change how you experience your life. In many ways the energy of your memories is more real than the energy of the berry you are about to eat.

"Those memories can make you smile with joy; they can make you salivate with hunger, they can start your entire body anticipating all that is to come. All of those memories are simply energy. Energy your mind calls up and filters in the same way it filters what is before you.

"The process is the same no matter what plane you exist on or what filter you experience existence through. It is not just the physical you interact with. It is the energy. Humanity is just one of many lenses in which the energy of existence is filtered through."

"If energy is life, how long does it last?"

"Energy is eternal. It can never be created or destroyed, it can only change form.

"The more energy you give to something the larger the impact it can have on your existence. The larger the impact, the more ripples are created and the wider the circle of energy becomes.

"You do not have to look at yourself to see this. Look to those things that you have appreciated in your life. Each of those people is just energy. It was you who kept them alive for yourself.

"The art you Love and appreciate is a reflection of the energy the artist imparted into that piece. The music that touches you is a reflection of the artist through the instrument they play. The books you read and feel touched by were written with the same energy that a photographer feeds into the images they capture. It is not the image that connects you to the artist you revere, it is the energy found within. Their art is simply a conduit for their energy.

"The more energy that was put into their work increases the connection those works carry. Artist, muse, landscape, patron. The work is the drop. Its ripples are the experiences each of us takes.

"This process of appreciation is a mirror for all of existence. Your very being is a web of connections in so many ways. You effect others in the same way the effect you. Humanity teaches you to connect to your own energy to the energy of others in whatever form it takes. When you feel drawn towards different people or animals, to food or to art, even to something as simple as a pebble, you are connecting to its energy, past, present and future.

"The impact that each object has in your life depends on the energy you empower it with. How much energy you give depends on how open you permit yourself to stay each experience and connection you have made. These are the lessons you will carry with you forever.

"It is why so much of human history has been devoted to capturing energy in whatever form it takes. In your heart, you sense the immense power that is possible with the pure energy that is. It opens your eyes as makes you realize the limitations of the energy that is against what could be. 'Oh,' you say 'if only you could tap into the rest...' "

"Does it matter what form the energy arrives in?"

He seemed to look up as he smiled at me. "Tomorrow," was all he said.

"Is that all?" I asked. A panic rose within me that I would lose him altogether.

He would have been shaking his head no if he were anything else. He didn't have to. It was enough.

"Digest what you have. We will speak when you have let our conversation settle. You will have questions, and we will have time."

I turned to look at the ocean that was all around us. It was only for a moment and I became deeply aware that there was more than just the rise and fall of the waves.

I watched the phosphorescence glow in gentle shades of green beneath the surface. I watched the waves, individual yet part of an endless carpet that merged and folded onto itself. They were not just something to see. They were to be felt.

Each rise and fall of a wave lifted and settled the boat in an endless motion. In time I was no longer aware of the boat. Instead, my body swayed back and forth on the energy and the gentle rocking that was. It was if I were in a cradle being rocked to sleep in my dream.

At some point I was no longer on the boat. I was floating on an ocean lost in time and space. Then my eyes closed. I still do not know when it was, but in my dream I became part of that

sensual motion of the sea, as if I were a part of the ocean itself.

SECOND DAY

There was a point in the night when the gentle lapping of the waves transformed into the rustling of olive branches. The creaks and groans of the mast became the sounds of goats wandering through the hills.

Through it all, the feeling of calm carried over from dream to waking. The comfort of that small craft was in the simplicity of the house. The ease of the ocean was nestled into the hills of the island. My mind had found a way to connect each together. Was this the connecting energy my companion spoke of?

My eyes cleared with the morning light. The rough goat bells clanged. The trees swayed. It was a rhythm known to the island and to my dream. Perhaps it was locked into the stiff-kneed walk of the goats. Perhaps it was ingrained in the way the cats moved about. Perhaps it was simply the ebb and flow of the island.

I listened. The pattern was there. I knew it was. I just couldn't find it. I couldn't put the rhythm to paper. It was left to the clockwork of the Universe on a more intricate level than I could discern.

My wife slept as the sun rose. Her head was buried into the pillow beside me as if on a cloud. I lay there and watched her as a gentle breeze lifted the curtains and welcomed them into our room.

The breeze filled my nose with the scent of olives and citrus. It filled my mind with images of exotic lands even though I knew they were right there just outside the window.

I remember somehow feeling lighter that morning. It was as if part of me were still floating on that boat. In time I began to recall the details of my dream. Each word carried a bit of mystery and wonder with it. I realized then that our languages were not the same. It was this that made me find my journal to write down what I could.

As I began to write I realized there were no words to describe the layering beneath our conversation. I realized neither of us had actually spoken a word, that our understanding was on another level. It seemed more of a transference of thoughts and memories and emotions that made our conversation more vivid than words could ever describe.

As I unpeeled our conversation into layers that I could put a pen to I felt as if a weight was being lifted from me. It was as if my skin were not encumbered with the realizations of life and the worries of the mundane. I was free to be wondrously aware of everything that was going on around me; touched but unconcerned.

I found my breath as I found the words. With each breath my body settled into itself and into the pillow beneath my head. With each breath I felt myself more grounded into the white sheets, more aware of the connections that were all around. With each breath out I felt lighter, easier, less reliant on my body and the world around me.

I wondered if this was what it felt like to have an umbilical cord, to be still in the womb. I felt connected to my dream and the universe, yet still aware of my body and myself. I was an individual, yet part of the whole. I was without the me.

Throughout the day my dream floated into and out of my consciousness. Or perhaps it was me floating in and out of my dream. I was in a café listening to the conversations that drifted past our table. I was more aware of the emotions that lay behind the words than the words themselves. It was a remarkable experience to know that this had always been there, I had just never been aware of them.

I was a part of it all but sat just outside the flow. I felt the tides that lived just below the intent and saw that everyone seemed to follow it regardless of their words without realizing it.

Behind our table a breakwater protected the small harbor. The waves pushed against it with a greenish blue hue. Each hid and revealed the rocks of the harbor wall with the gentle rise and fall of the waves. Perhaps one in three waves made it past the entrance. The boats responded to their gentle nudges. Their masts swayed. The world went on.

Further out several boats moved imperceptibly against the horizon. Their sails were full white canopies, but to me they were small arcs against the sky. They were too far out for me to measure their wake. I wondered if that is what we looked like to those sitting in the café of my dream - if it was a dream at all.

As everyone started to pass the small dishes of olives and fish past me, I picked up a napkin and let go of my experience. My dream passed into the distance as I joined the conversation and the moment I was in.

That afternoon we rented a boat and motored to the beaches that spotted the island where it met the sea. The coves these spots created were where we dropped our anchor. We watched as it sank into the clear water and swam to the beaches. The sun, the sandy grains, even the rocks were welcoming.

As the sun arced down our attention shifted to thoughts of the evening. I could feel more than the earth spinning on its axis as the sun slowly set and the sea settled into night.

It made me aware of how tremendously big it all was, how old it all was, and how infinitely small and young we were within it. No, not small and young, but a wonderful part of the enormity that was.

We returned to Corinne's house, our hands filled with bags from the market. There was a collective excitement for what was to come. We were inspired by the simple dishes of the cafes and each of us took turns putting together and serving our own versions to each other. Wine was passed and conversations were shared. Each was a taste of the life that we were all enjoying.

The walls of her home disappeared. The living room opened onto the deck and the deck onto the roof. There was no end or beginning to her home. Each simply flowed into the next with the food and the wine and the conversation connected them all. We simply floated above the world on that flat white roof, touching down momentarily to plate another dish or to refill our glasses.

Around us a chorus of cicadas sang. Above us the constellations crawled across the black sky, and we in turn spun in our own orbits around the house. Each in our own slow march to dawn. It was as if we were at the center of all creation, suspended on that white roof as the Universe spun wildly above us and below. The horizon had long since disappeared with the sun. We were alone in our togetherness.

I realized I hadn't mentioned my dream to anyone. Not because it wasn't at the top of my mind but because I was still processing it. My mind was playing through the ways we connected over and over again. Before bed I read my notes and played through the details of the night before. I realized I had not gotten it all down. I smiled as I doubted I ever would.

I realized the details weren't to be found in the texture of the boat or the grain of the wood. It was found in the intent each of us conveyed to the other. There was nothing specific about what he said. There was something very specific about his intentions, as if the details were found in his movements and gestures.

It all came together for me as a distinct impression. What he communicated was a wonderful symphony in which the words were only a tiny part. The result was infinitesimally specific and magnificently all encompassing at the same time.

As the night buzzed around me, I could see his intent in the rhythms of the people, the dinner, the roof and the way in which the world came together. It was fluid and solid at the same time. There was a resonance to the night just as there was in him. Each movement vibrated with meaning on an invisible level I could not yet see.

The boundary that defined him was the same boundary that defined the evening. None of it was distinct. Each was a fluid area of activity. There was no start and stop to any of it. There was no border. There was simply an area of greater and lesser probability that constantly moved and carried whatever energy that was along with it.

It was with that realization that I said my goodnights and finally laid my head on my pillow. I drifted off to sleep with a smile of what the day had brought and what my sleep would bring.

The idea that none of this was real, and that nothing we knew was 100% solid was suspended in my mind. The thought that life was nothing more than a series of possibilities. That our existence was our perception of being rather than our physical states, and that the reality of our existence was based on the energy of what we gave rather than what we took.

I was comfortable with the uncertainty of it all, as well as with the perfection that lay in the imperfection of its ebb and flow.

SECOND NIGHT

On Love And The Singularity of Existence

Where do evenings stop and dreams begin? The only answer I could find that night is everywhere and nowhere. There are no hard edges to the universe or to existence. There is no black and white. There is just a sinuous flow through the shades of whatever color you are looking at. That is how all things are in life. There are no absolutes. There are so many factors that everything is a fluid variable that only sets in the here and now.

It is why we never really begin or end a dream. Instead, we drop into them as if surfing a wave. We feel the swell before we realize the wave is here. We paddle to bring ourselves into the lift and drop in on them somewhere midstream. And then we ride them for as long as we can, or risk having them crash upon us.

The memorable dreams of my life floated in and out on a tide of consciousness. I have watched entire sets of dreams pass, waiting for the right one before I paddled to catch it and ride it for as long as I could, or as long as it would permit me to.

My mind may search for a dream's origin. But there isn't any. Each dream comes in on the tail-end of the dream before it. Behind it another dream follows. It may be minutes or hours between dreams, but that time is meaningless until our consciousness brings it into focus.

That night there was a fuzzy border between my waking world and that of my dreams. It was as if I was in the turbulence between two planes, trying to find the right set of waves before paddling into one.

My second dream never really began. I'm not even sure when I slipped past the border of sleep or if I was even dreaming at all. At some point I was simply on the boat.

I knew I had sailed past the harbor, but I don't remember when. It was like that moment when you come back into awareness behind the wheel of a car after driving for miles without being aware of how far you'd gone. You know you'd been driving, but you can't remember a single landmark you passed. You just know you'd been driving for a while.

At sea when there is no destination and no real markers to reference, it is especially difficult. When there are only rolling waves every direction begins to look the same.

I turned to see the lights of the small harbor fade into the night behind me. At first the lights ignited the stones of the breakwater in a soft glow. Then the stones disappeared in a slow roll as we rose and surfed down the waves. The jetty reappeared for me one last time. It gave me the assurance I needed. Then, as the stern dipped over the peak of a blue/black wave, it was gone.

I was anxious in my dream. Glad to be back but wanting something solid to hold onto. I reached out to check the condition and safety of our boat. I pulled on the lines about me testing their tautness. I wiggled a belaying pin and gently pushed the tiller back and forth.

I was comforted by how well she rode the wind and the waves. I looked up, satisfied that the sail had filled out against the following wind and sea. For some reason I decided to take my dream more seriously than I had the night before. As if I had innately decided it was more than a dream. I now felt somehow responsible for the boat and how well she was tended. I did not want the next voyager to find her wanting.

I noted that my course was a few points before the wind and a few points off of the waves. It let my sail comfortably out to one side and gave us a light heel. I rested my hand on the tiller, but I barely needed to guide the weathered wood. Instead it tugged gently with the roll of each wave, as if it knew the course to follow.

This time I saw my passenger before he joined me in the cockpit. He stood out on the water like a buoy riding the waves. His feet were beneath the surface. He seemed to move up and down with the waves around him, as if he was weighted to the sea below, as if his foundation was with the water itself.

He was solid and stable as he gently bobbed with the sea around him. His serene air let me know he was comfortable and not needing a rescue in any way.

I did not adjust my course or steer toward him. I knew our courses would intersect no matter what I did.

I pulled the tiller just a hair and the boat responded. It was more to signal my intentions than anything else. It was an invitation for him to join me.

As I sailed past him, he less climbed on board as much as he simply was on board. He was just there, sitting across from me as if he had always been there. His feet were tucked beneath him. His back was planted against the wood and the two of us were in mid-conversation as if there had been no pause in our thoughts from the night before. Our conversation continued as if it had never ended.

"Is this the ebb and flow of existence?" I asked pointing to the sea and to him and his entry.

"It is," he said, smiling without smiling.

"The energy that is you has a very long journey before it. Along the way you will find your place as you find yourself. When you do you will find it in the sea you are already a part of.

"Before that moment of true awakening there are infinite points of awareness and enlightenments to behold. Each one gives such unbelievable Love and joy that each is a destination unto itself. Each one is finite and yet infinite.

"To understand existence is to understand that the finite is the infinite. It is to view existence as an endless ocean where waves rebound in an eternal flow of energy. To understand that is to expand your consciousness beyond linear thought.

"A ripple starts when a pebble is dropped into the ocean. That ripple does not extend in just one direction. It expands in all directions. It builds with the energy it gathers from each point of consciousness it encounters. It transforms with each experience it passes through. It evolves into a wave created from the energy of experience.

"To understand existence is to understand that a wave never stops. It never stands still. It endlessly changes form and direction based on the energy it comes into contact with. The end of one wave is the beginning of the next.

"A single wave may seem solitary on its own until you see the impact it has on the wave behind it and the wave before it. Wavelets are formed and the ocean as a whole is shaped by all of the connections that single wave brings with it.

"It is less the size of the wave that matters. It is the connections that wave brings with it to every other point in the ocean and beyond that matters. In that, it is the vantage point from which you witness that wave that makes the difference.

"From up close you may only see a wave. From far away the wave looks small amidst the current of waves around it. From further still, the wave is no more. It is the ocean that matters.

"No matter the size, a single wave effects everything as it travels through the sea of existence. It changes every wave it touches. Its energy effects those that it does not touch directly.

"You are no different from that wave. Your thoughts, your actions and your energy effect everything and everyone around you. You affect people who you have never even met or touched in person. It is why when you change your energy you change the world and the energy of existence as well."

I pictured the map of the world and the oceans between the continents. I didn't see endless waves. I saw the boundaries we have all been taught to see.

"What happens when the wave hits the shore?"

"The energy of that wave never hits the shore. It passes through it. Sea and water are physical planes of existence. There is turbulence where they meet the shore. But the energy? It passes through unyielding.

"It is very human to create boundaries. They reflect the limits of the human experience. You compartmentalize the space you are in to see it as you see yourself - a physical being. But what of the energy beneath? Is that not part of the human experience as well?

"When you search for boundaries you define existence based on your own limitations. You see water and land without stepping back to see the larger existence that is all around you.

"The energy of a wave does not stop when a wave crashes upon the sand. It reverberates and continues. Its mists feed the vines and the trees. Its energy continues to change mountains, but it does not stop.

"With every boundary you create there is an entire universe through which the energy moves. There is turbulence where planes meet. Smaller waves may burst from that turbulence and from that point of connection. But the connection does not stop, neither does the energy.

"The energy of the oceans create the clouds. Where those clouds strike mountains their rain brings life to the ground. The impact of the oceans extend well beyond the beaches that define the sea. The tremors each wave creates as it crashes on the beach continue on. The waves you see in the water are merely reflections of the energy they ride upon.

"Every wave builds and crests on its journey, but it does not stop. It joins new currents. It is deflected by rocks and mountains. It becomes part of the larger wave that continues on.

"The energy does not cease to exist because you no longer see it. It is you who must look beyond your own sense of comfort to see the connection that is. Water turns to mist. Mist waters plants. Salt and sand is deposited or removed to create a beach or to bring that beach back to the ocean. Waves redefine the land and the sky and the water is in turn defined by it.

"Change your perspective and you will see the energy beneath each wave as it continues through time and space. That is how you will find the connections of the universe and existence."

He seemed to pause in his thoughts and to smile in that non-smile of his.

"In truth you are no different. Just as a wave impacts the land before it, you impact the world before you. You impact so much more than you are aware of. Just as you are impacted by everything around you in return.

"A wave is shaped by each surface it strikes. You are shaped by each experience you endure. Just as you shape the world around you, each wave reshapes the world around it. Both of you are echoes of the energy beneath you. The energy of existence.

"The energy you experience on your journey is no different than the energy a wave experiences on its journey. You reflect and refract in new directions based on the energy that you exist in. The impact of that energy creates new waves that begin new journeys in new directions. Each is an echo of you. Each is a new opportunity. You leave behind a shoreline that is changed forever once you pass to find a new one.

"That is how existence works. That is how life works. You never cease to exist; you transform yourself and those around you through your experiences and your energy. Your journey continues, forever polishing your edges to fit with the energy of those around you.

"When your spirit evolves to the limit of your abilities it does not stop growing. Like a wave, it evolves and continues on to explore existence on new and different levels. Each experience is not better or worse than another. It is a new perspective through which to grow."

Step back and let go, I reassured myself. I gave myself permission and found myself content with the endless flow of existence. There are no solid boundaries to struggle with, just the smooth form of raindrops and the never ending flow of water.

"Is experiencing existence firsthand the only way to learn how it all works?"

"If you want to witness the mechanics of existence all you have to do is look around you. They are not hard to see. They are mirrored in every step you take. They are mirrored in the actions of nature and the structure of atoms. They are simple. They are the same for everyone and everything. Simply look beyond the surface and you will see the patterns in true nature. They are the constant. They never vary. Those are the rules of existence.

"A drop of water and an entire ocean behave the same way. The difference is infinitesimally small. They obey the same laws of physics and nature. They respond in the same way to outside forces. What makes them different, their size, their shape, their mass, is due to your perspective than to their nature.

"Step back and you will quickly find that existence does not discriminate. There are no biases or special rules that only apply to a select few. Just as the law of gravity applies equally to all things, the laws of existence apply to everybody and everything, both physically and metaphysically.

"Every wave and every leaf responds to the wind in the same way. Those same rules are echoed in the stars above and the earth below. You simply have to slow down and step back to see those patterns as they are, free from your own fears of what you think should be.

"A single drop of water behaves the way it does because it is part of existence. The physical laws that cause a raindrop to dance and spin as it falls apply to the way a galaxy twists and turns as it travels through the universe.

"The laws that cause that raindrop to flow from a pond to a river, and to the sea are the same laws that cause an ocean to follow the moon and the moon to follow a planet.

"The laws that guide a lioness to care for her cub are the same that guide a parent to Love their child. If you do not see this look within. Your consciousness mirrors the sea of existence no more or less than that of a drop of water. When your spirit expands to the limits of your body it does not stop. It continues to expand to find new limits. Your spirit discovers new wonders just as a drop of water flows into new bodies of water.

"Each grows and evolves along its journey. Each purifies itself until it has shed everything that has held it back. The moment it does this it finds that the simplest and purist form of its actions is also the most enlightened.

"In every life there is a time when growth is no longer the goal. Simplicity is. One cycle diminishes and another expands. The largest wave fractures into smaller ones without ceasing to be. Each wavelet begins its own journey of discovery. Each discovers a new cycle with which to begin on its own. Each grows and evolves until the sea is once again calm."

"When you see beyond your self-limiting senses you begin to see the patterns of the universe and of existence. Every move echoes the moves of another. There is no mystery to it. Cause and effect.

"The more you seek, the more you will see. Every time you recognize the patterns you will smile knowing that the energy of existence is behind it all. You will be comforted knowing that existence is truly simple if you allow it to be.

"Learn how a raindrop responds to the forest and you will understand how an ocean responds to the wind, how a galaxy to the universe, and how a universe to the ebb and flow of existence. Each is simply an echo of the energy of Love.

"There are no special dispensations. There is no bias. There are no exceptions. There are just the mechanics of existence, and they are simple. They only seem complex because the expanse appears so vast."

We sat there for a bit, he motionless against the movements of the boat, I reeling in his thoughts, alive with his energy.

It was my thoughts that betrayed me. Or should I say the waves of energy my thoughts created that gave my intent away? They found their way out. They seemed to create ripples on their own before I could edit them.

"You mentioned the energy of Love. Is this the energy of the Universe?" my mind seemed to say.

"The energy of existence is the purest and simplest of all energies. It is what all other energy is derived from and eventually returns to. It is the energy that holds everything in creation together. It is creation.

"It is Love. In the end, what can be purer or simpler than Love?

"Love is the force behind gravity that brings planets together. Love sparks the light and burns the fires of the sun and stars. Love unites all things as one and energizes the voids that separate the universes into life.

"Where there is Love worlds are created. Where there is none, the fabric of existence pulls apart. Without Love all things unravel and drift alone. Without Love there is a void of nothingness.

" The same is true for all people and all creation. Look around and you will see this is true throughout your human experience. When you find Love, when you fall in Love with someone, you cannot help but think of them even when they are worlds away. You yearn to be with them in body, mind and spirit. There is a connection that transcends time and space.

"When they are with you, you feel complete. When they are not their energy remains in your thoughts. When they drift out of your thoughts, that is when you feel empty and truly alone.

"When you are in Love you can touch the energy of the Universe within you and without. When you are in Love you want to share that feeling of completeness. You want to create a family. You want to create art and poetry. You want the world to be as beautiful as you have found yourself to be.

"This is the energy that fills the sea of existence. It is Love that is behind the energy of all things. Love creates the ebb and flow of being. It is why all of existence is so simple to understand once you open yourself to Love."

"What about those who have no Love?" I thought?

"Everyone has Love. Not everyone is open to it.

"When people are closed no Love they feel the emptiness of the void that surrounds them. They are unaware of the waves of energy that pass by them for they cannot travel through the void of existence. There is nothing for the energy of existence to travel through. At their core they feel their loneliness.

"With that loneliness comes fear. Their fear turns to anger and darkness. They recoil and try to make the world around them as dark and as bleak as the void before them.

"This is how the wheels of existence turn. We bathe in a sea of Love. It is all around you. It passes through you. All you have to do is open yourself up to the Love that is. It is there for you.

"Love is no different within the human experience. You simply see it through the lens that you create for yourself.

"When you smile people smile back. When you are angry people avoid you like the void you are in. The beautiful truth is mirrored on every level of existence. There is a single energy echoed in all things. That energy is Love."

"This should not be a surprise to you. You already know it to be true. The Love you have within you flows from the Love of existence. It is the same Love that flows through you and around you. It creates a circuit for you to complete, if you wish to.

"The Love you carry in your heart passes into the world and the universe around you. It passes into all of existence. That is why the Love you have effects the way you feel. It effects the way everyone around you feels. It effects how you see the world.

"You see it in the way the people and animals respond to you. The waves of existence that pass through you connect you with everyone and everything that is. It is the waves of Love that deliver your energy outward in all directions and to every level of existence. It is through Love that you change the world and heal the voids that fray the sea of existence."

"Look around. When there is Love in the Universe stars are created and galaxies expand. It is as if the collective consciousness speaks – Let There Be Light. Where there is a lack of Love, existence frays, the light fades and dark holes appear.

"New Universes are created every second. Each is held together by the Love that is all around us and within us. Just as the human brain changes in response to the world it experiences, existence is transformed by the energy it experiences.

"The Love you feel fuels the stars, generates the attraction of gravity and powers the strong and weak forces which keep everything together. When the energy is strong wondrous things occur. Where the energy is diluted, existence pulls apart. Love is like everything in existence because it is existence. Love does not favor the few or the worthy. It is there for everyone and everything."

I could not help but watch as my mind sorted through every Love I had ever had and those I had not. They brought to mind how the feelings remained long after we had parted. I even thought back to how I felt when our Love had fallen apart.

I remembered a break up on the side of a Los Angeles highway as the rain poured down my windshield. I remembered how the world fell apart when I heard those words 'it just wasn't working.'

I also remembered that wonderful feeling of invincibility when Love appeared in the lightest of breezes, a glass in her hand and the magic energy of an instant connection.

I hesitated to ask because it sounded childish to me, but there it was in my head before I could stop it, "when people fall in Love are stars truly created?"

"Yes, they are. Let go of the wall between the physical and the metaphysical. There is only turbulence where those two planes intersect.

"When two people find Love you say that sparks ignite. That is a reflection of how the Universe responds to the energy that is there. In that moment a new circuit is completed and it all fits together seamlessly. Energy is harnessed at the deepest level. The excess energy is sent out in the sparks that fly. It must go somewhere; remember energy can never be created or destroyed, it can only change form.

"When the energies of the Universe come together wonderful things happen. It is not that energy is created, it is concentrated to a degree where it can no longer be contained.

"That energy explodes in the beautiful creation of a child or a star. Both are the same event experienced from different vantage points. When two people find the Love that exists between them, they feel as if they were meant to be. They fit together in perfect balance. They become whole. They create a wonderful life. It is not coincidence this happens. It is echoed at every level of existence. It is the way of existence.

"When the Love between two people is diluted, the bond that held their existence together unravels. When it unravels beyond a point, their life together, their world together, disappears. A void between them opens. A void of understanding is created. That void can only be healed by reaching across the emptiness to replace the fear and the anger that is, with Love.

"When the energies of Love fail to connect and come together as they once did, the fabric of existence begins to unravel. More gaps occur. More voids appear that prevent the flow of energy and of Love.

"It is no different between two people as it is on an existential scale. Water flows from high to low as it seeks a balance. Air flows from high pressure to low as it seeks balance. The sea of Love that we all exist in does the same. The flow of Love creates the never ending current we all exist in.

"Our Love seeks balance and continuity free of voids. It is the way of everything. Balance is simply the natural order of all things, at every level of existence."

I pictured a sea of Love and light where the energy sparkled and flowed freely. I saw the voids that formed the gaps between the points of consciousness that were. There was a darkness to them. A lack of color that is not visible but that we know is there. It is the same feeling we have when we look out and absolutely nothing comes back. Not even feelings.

"Is the void you spoke of what Hell looks like?"

"There is no Hell. There is only Love. Where there is no Love there is emptiness. Hell is simply one way one person described the unfathomable.

"Anger, hate, fear, these are emotions that have been used to describe a lack of Love. Each is a very human emotion that is used to describe a place that is so void of everything that it is impossible to describe. When you try to place boundaries and rules to something that has none, you change the nature of it. You turn it into an object when in truth it has no form."

"Love is all around you. Love is everywhere. You simply have to open yourself up and allow it to flow in. This does not mean saying yes to everything. It is done by managing your fears and your ego so that you can welcome the Love of others. You do this by offering Love. Love is there to anyone who opens up. All you have to do is reach out and invite Love to flow in.

"This is not just for people. This is true of plants and stones. Even places have Love within them. The sacred nature of an object exists because this stone or that mountain has an abundance of energy that reflects your own. It exists because you have opened yourself up to receiving the Love that flows.

"When you find a sacred place you feel a connection. You allow your energy to flow through whatever is in front of you. That object will never shut off the connection you feel. It is yours to feed, if you wish.

"The opposite of this experience is found in those places devoid of Love, places where the Love of existence is blocked from flowing. It is a weakness in the fabric of existence where no connection has been found. It is a place where nothing exists.

"The void is empty of warmth and understanding, but it can be healed. A single strand of Love can be thrown across. A smile or a kind word. That is the bridge upon which an entire connection can be built.

"With each strand of Love you begin to weave a web of energy. As you do you also learn to purify your own energy. You refine the edges of your consciousness until your consciousness fits into all of the other points of consciousness without end.

"This is how you become balanced. This is how existence becomes balanced. It is done with Love, until all of existence is an endless sea free of gaps and voids of separation."

"If there is a *why* to your journey, even to existence, this is a part of it. As you become aware of the divinity in yourself, you become aware of the divinity in all things. As you do, you gain a better understanding of what Love truly is. You learn to bring Love together so that you can join the Love that is all around and continue the flow of energy that balances all of existence.

"When you learn how to join with other drops without losing yourself, you learn how to be one in a sea of Love. That is the moment that you understand to ride the currents of energy throughout the ocean of existence.

"When you see the patterns in all things. You learn to understand its currents and the nature of its waves. That is the moment you see the divinity in all things.

"When you see the divinity within you, you will open a window to the way of the Universe and all of creation."

My mind started, "If there are no borders and everything moves toward balance how do we remain individuals in this sea of Love?"

He seemed to shimmer in a smile as I received his thoughts.

"A sea of Love paints a beautiful image, but the truth is more than an image. It is a state in which your consciousness radiates in more directions than there are in the universe. There are textures and layers and states of mind that are beyond all that you can imagine. Each is its own point on the existential compass that is.

"No matter what plane you view existence from or what world you inhabit, whatever reality you are experiencing is simply an echo, an impression of the energy that is there. The energy of Love is the medium that your consciousness exists in.

"Every emotion you have echoes a separate plane of existence. Every experience you take pleasure in is a wave that radiates out like the ripple from the drop of the pebble, an echo of the original event that was."

His voice seemed to trail off into the clouds before he began again.

"You are in the sea of Love right now. You are in a current of Love that flows around you and through you. When you open yourself up to it, that current fills you and provides for you.

"You feel it when you are a part of it. That is the moment when there is nothing you cannot do, when you have endless energy and endless opportunities. That is the moment you realize that there is nothing more than the pure energy of Love.

"What you see and hear and feel at that moment is the eternal energy of Love, not viewed through the lens of humanity, but witnessed from within, as a part of it. From the vantage point of being rather than viewing. Know that the is all around you at all times. It is up to you to stay open to it.

"In so many ways the world you live in is like the boat that we float in. The difference is you are more than floating on the water around you. You are part of the water. You are the water.

"When you are open the currents flow around you and through you. They keep you afloat and support you with the pure energy of Love. That is when a single point becomes the infinite. When the sea is both endless and is you. It is the moment when the walls of a raindrop disappear, making it a part of the sea it has entered.

"Give yourself permission to open up to it and you will grow and expand to eternity. You will see the limitlessness of yourself and of everything that is.

"The choice is yours. You can close yourself off from the energy that you are a part of. You can try to remain forever in the body that you are comfortable in until it wastes away. Or you can reach out and embrace all of the joy and Love that is.

"One is the path of fear. The other is the path of openness. One shrinks back into the very elements it rose from, the other helps you expand and become so much more than you are. It is evolution on every level."

I am not even sure if I nodded or simply felt the words become accepted at the core of my being. But he knew. He responded with thoughts of his own before I even asked.

"You are an echo of your own consciousness. Your energy exists in the sea of energy that is all around you. You are a part of all the energy that is. You only see a narrow slice of existence because you see it through the lens of the human experience. Know that everything you experience is a reverberation of the energy that is you.

"When you feel Love it is because your true self has been washed over by a wave of Love. When you connect with someone, it is because your true self has found a connection in the currents of energy that flow around you and through you.

"When you find Love your world feels complete because it is complete. When you lose Love you feel incomplete because you are incomplete. When you search for Love again and again, it is because you know it is there for you.

"You will inevitably find it. That is not in question. What your journey will be along the way and what experiences you will explore are what make you unique. The journey each of us experiences as we explore our own existence is what existence is all about."

I looked away and saw the sea. The endless rolling of the waves. The gentle transfer of energy from wave to wave and from wave to the rocking of our boat. There was an invisible connection to it all that became visible once I acknowledged it.

"…and is God the gardener of this sea?"

"If you more comfortable with that image, then so be it. What you call God is the energy of Love. The way they interact is the way they interact. "No matter what name you decide to call the energy, it will forever be Love.

"Your greatest prophets preached a single idea - that of Love. It was only after they passed their idea of eternal Love on that the rest of humanity manifested it into a being.

"Whatever name you wish to call the eternal Love that is within you and without you. Just know that by whatever word you are most comfortable, that will not make it any more or less real. Just know that the energy of God is Love, and that Love will forever be within you. That Love is you.

Jeff Cannon

"If you wish to accept God in everything that is, then simply accept everything that is. If you wish to accept God as the creator for all that is, then simply accept the moment of creation that is in every moment. If you see God as a union of all the laws of the natural universe, then simply accept the laws of the universe for what they are. Just do not judge another for seeing it another way, because at the basis of it all is the energy of Love.

"The way you bless the world around you is to witness the world around you in everything that you do. See beyond yourself and remain open to all that is. When you do, you bless all that is.

"Acknowledge your life by simply living your life. That is all you need to do to reach the divine. When you do that you begin to understand existence amid the enormity of what is. If you are ever in doubt, step back and you will find faith everywhere.

You will find faith in your sacred halls of science. You will come to understand that science is God in so many ways. In the end your belief in science or in God is one and the same. Each relies on the faith you carry. Your faith is what reverberates throughout you and the world around you .

"Science points to the Big Bang as the point in which the Universe was created. Before that moment there was neither space nor time. It is the moment of Creation, a point where consciousness came into being. It is no different than hearing the words, 'Let there be light.' It is no different than a raven dropping a seed into the sea of existence, or any of the other creation myths that every person has brought into the light.

"It it no different than the Hopi sending a water beetle to bring back mud from beneath the waves. Even the staunchest scientists will agree, that no matter what direction you approach it from, it is impossible to imagine that event. How long did it last without time existing? How large was it without space?

"Can you picture what occurred in that fraction of a non-existent nanosecond? It was an event that remains so far beyond your comprehension, so powerful, that who is to say how it was all created?

"At the moment of creation even science disappears into faith. The big bang is a moment where formulas no longer apply and calculations no longer make sense. At that infinitesimal point even researchers have nothing more than to ask for faith to prove their concepts.

"From observation to religion to science, each relies on faith when it come to understanding how the universe was created.

"The one constant beneath it all, is that at some point in existence all of this came into being from noting. Just as you did."

"At some point people saw the forces of the Universe as it was. They viewed the world around them as something to exist in. The weather, the seasons, the act of Love were all simply a part of the ever turning wheel of existence.

"The stars in the heavens were a reminder of the vastness of the universe. Those became a backdrop for the theater of life.

"In time people noticed how the stars turned above them. They questioned how day became night and asked how tides and seasons repeated themselves with such regularity.

"Unable to imagine that existence simply was, they created entities to give each meaning. They created images of animals and people to give order to what was already there. They were simply trying to make sense of the world around them.

"In all this time, it has not changed. There is simply one Love and one God who reflects that Love to all of humanity. Even with that single God, people cannot stop observing nature as it is. Science continues to test theories with observations. The world is no longer flat. It is no longer the center of existence. Even the physical matter we once thought so solid is shown to be ephemeral. Science and religion are not in conflict. They simply ask for your faith in different ways.

"Even science is giving way to the reality that the lines between the physical and metaphysical are no longer quite so distinct. The complexities of science are showing that everything works in a beautiful flow of energy.

"T here is, once again, a simple beauty to all that is. Proving how it all began is less important than the simple fact that it was created, and that point of creation, continues to evolve based on the laws of nature. Just like you.

"It is as if a giant circle is just now being completed. As with all things in existence, you depart on a journey only to return back to where you started. The difference is that you are more aware after your journey. Your consciousness has grown, and you see existence from a new vantage point. In the end what you find is that beneath the veneer it is still Love that fuels it all.

"For some God is a word used to describe everything in the Universe. For others, God is a word that explains what they are unable to comprehend themselves. For still others, God reflects the fear they have for what is.

"On one level the idea behind God is a combination of all the physical laws that gives order to life. On another level, God is a reflection of the energy of Love that is found within everything.

"Either way God is a part of you and you are a part of God. The spirit you see in God is a reflection of the spirit within yourself. That is because God's spirit comes from within you. It is you.

"It is why there is no judgment day waiting for you at the end of this life. Whatever judgment you have is found within you. You create your own judgment all on your own. This is also why you can choose to un-create it if you wish.

"Every day you judge yourself you create your own heaven and your own hell through the lenses of regret, anger, self-loathing, and hatred you see life through. You can do just the opposite by seeing life through the filter of Love."

"You see, God is not found in a book. God is found within the ever expanding consciousness of humanity. From seeing the divine in nature, to finding the Divine within yourself, that is the true evolution of self. It is proving spirituality through science and bringing the physical and the metaphysical together.

"There is a creator energy. There is also a personal energy that is part of your journey and your evolution. They exist side by side on the same plane because they both come from the same place. You simply have to stay open to see existence as it truly is. Free from bias and human need."

His was an explanation that mirrored the patterns of the Universe. It fit with my own feelings of what is and what could be. It was a thread that I saw connecting everything at every level. It simply made sense.

Once again the thoughts seemed to fly from my mind without the substance of words to support them. I was whole and complete in my body, mind and spirit. And that was good.

"Then where does religion come into play?" I asked.

"Are you referring to the religion of fear or the religion of Love?

"The only religion you need is that of witnessing the Universe as it is. By whatever name you wish to use, God is all around you. God is within you. God is Love. God is you. You simply need to open up to see the patterns that are within you and without you.

"In those patterns the nature of all things will be found. The interactions in a drop of water are the same as those of a galaxy. Atoms and solar systems move in the same way because they are born of the same energy. They are one. They are Love.

"We are all driven by and toward the same ends; Love. That is where God is found. Not in somebody's writings, but within each of us."

There was a pause that seemed to last a lifetime. He gazed through me to the horizon that was behind. He watched the waves that crested beyond my eyes.

He smiled what I perceived to be a forlorn smile and then spoke. "I am sorry. But I am tired." It was all he said. "Sleep in your waking and we will speak again when you wake to your dreams."

For a moment I thought to say something. But there was nothing to say. At that moment I felt as if I were empty. Drained, as if I was seeing myself through his eyes.

I was vacant and without form. It was enough to make me lie back in an open self-awareness. I was the thinnest of thin vessels that barely separated what was within and what was without.

It was not an uncomfortable feeling. Quite the opposite. It was a freeing feeling of complete belonging. I knew that I was nothing, not even an impediment to the ebb and flow of all that was around me.

I was nothing. But in the briefest of glimmers, I was everything.

THIRD DAY

That morning I woke to the sun and the roosters. The cicadas were out singing to the clanging of the soft bells. Each layered the hills with textures of sound and life.

I lay there in the calm cacophony of the island, taking it all in as the land woke up around me. I could feel the resonance of the thousand-year-old olive trees. I missed my dream, I missed the feel of the boat and the ebb and flow of the water, but I was content to be back in the world as I knew it.

On the outside it was a simple life of cats and goats and olives, of the beaches and the sun. Beneath that veneer my mind was alive with the words my friend had shared with me, that I continued to share with myself. My thoughts were alive with the network of existence that was all around me.

I rose to find I was alone in the house. The others were there, but their energy was still wrapped in the quiet of sleep. It was as if a low-level hum drifted through the rooms. It was the energy of people. It was there.

I savored that energy as I tiptoed into the living room. I knew the sound of tea being brewed and coffee being steeped would fill the house with shaggy heads and drifting forms.

They would chide me for the sarong I was wearing with a raised eyebrow or a smirk, but never a word. It was what I chose to wear and they accepted it as if it were Chanel.

I knew the silence would evolve into the sounds of us piling into our little jeep and heading into town. My mouth salivated with the thought of our dockside taverna. My mind clicked to life with the thought of food and sun and conversation. Of being alive as the world spun around us all.

I knew that would not happen for hours to come, and until that moment arrived I would be mindful to the quiet breathing of the house and the sun and the island of Ithaca.

The cool air rested on the olive trees as I opened the doors to the day. The air was not quite a breeze but it moved ever so gently. It moved lightly with the energy of the island itself.

I walked the narrow staircase to the deck outside with my tea. That staircase hugged the outer wall of the house in a way that you could not help but touch the bright white along the way.

The deck was empty. I sat at the head of the long rustic table and sipped from my mug. I sipped long and slow, tasting the nuances of my Assam as I followed the grain of the wood into the distance.

I watched the diamonds on the water sparkle all the way to the sun. Here and there a boat drew a white line across the greenish-blue water. Each line marked where it was coming from and where it was going to. The wakes they left behind were a direction but not a destination. A path along which their journey led.

I smiled. They had no idea that I was up here, watching them from my vantage point as I enjoyed my tea. They were focused on whatever destination they had in mind, unaware of anything outside their own little voyage.

It really did depend on your perspective, I thought.

Where the boat came from was the past. Where it was going to was the future. Where it was right now was what really mattered, and that was the present.

"How many vantage points are there in life?" I asked no one. "How many perspectives are there from which to see the world?"

My mind jumped. No matter how dark my sunglasses were they would never be dark enough for the dazzling white of

Corinne's house. All I could see was augmented by the bright white of the sun that bounced off the clay walls.

That white was echoed in the small square dots that climbed the mountains of each island. In each of those houses there was someone like me waking up and observing the brightness of their own little universe. Each of us unaware that there were other universes on other islands throughout the sea.

My universe that morning was found in the paint of the house. It was in the clay of my cup and the angle through which I followed the wake of the boats at sea.

There was so much white in my world that morning that it was almost painful. The house seemed to provide a glow that I could feel on my body and face. I could feel it through my sarong as it changed the color and the texture of the fabric itself.

I closed my eyes but the light was still visible through my eyelids. So much so that I smiled at the energy that I was basking in. Whether I looked directly at the house or not, it was still there. Whether I opened my eyes and squinted to see it in the houses across the water or not, it would still be there.

It was there in the way the figure in my dreams was there. He was a presence whether I looked at him or not. He remained with me through his energy; less a physical entity, more a glow.

It dawned on me that he was not an individual, but a collection. A sum of his parts. Just like the white of the islands he was everywhere, a subtext to my life whether I opened my eyes to him or not.

Later that day we wandered through the small town that was nearest us. I was aware of the jostling of people in the narrow market. The stalls of produce and products defined the potential for space, but it was the people and their energy that filled it.

It was not overly crowded. You could see areas of density in the mingling people. You could see areas of empty space that were quickly filled. I watched as a space opened up in the crowd. It quickly filled as people flowed into it.

Nobody was pushing or rushing one way or another. It was an easy flow of life that balanced itself from one gap to another. As one space became crowded people naturally stepped into the area around it.

It was the same ebb and flow that water followed. It flowed from areas of density to areas of emptiness. I had always seen the patterns but was never really aware of them. I now saw the ebb and flow of the Universe in something as simple and small as this market.

I looked into the sky and watched the birds. There were no clouds, but there was a pattern to their flight. It was the same pattern I saw in the market. It was the pattern of existence. From the unimaginable scale of the Universe, to the birds in the sky, to the market I stood in, the same rules applied.

It didn't matter if it was people or birds, air or water, it was simply the way the universe spun. It was a small moment of enlightenment that I watched come together.

As the morning flowed into afternoon, we spent our lunch at the little café we somehow always ended up in. It overlooked the harbor and the stone pilings that protected the boats within it. Plates of fish, grilled vegetables and hummus were passed around as we decided what to do for the rest of the day.

I was particularly hungry that day. It was as if I missed a meal somewhere. I puzzled over it for a moment, until I let it go. Instead thinking of energy and if I had somehow expended more in my thoughts and the dreams of the night.

That was the first time I felt a shudder run down my spine. I knew something temporal had shifted within me. I recognized the food on my plate. I saw the small buildings of the town as well as the hills and the sky above. But now I saw them in a different light. They were not just objects. They were points of connection. The same energy of the sun grew the vegetables and baked the bricks, also warmed the people that tilled the land and delivered the dishes.

There was a simple warmth that passed through everyone. There was a joy found in their smiles and laughter. It could be seen and heard in the conversation and the warmth they showed. There was an energy to the island that was lost in the cities of the world. No. Not lost. It was there. Just hidden in the layers of modern living.

Here there was no news. There were no greater goals or constructs. There was simply the here and now. There were the dishes and the wine, the sun and the sea, the today and the moment we were in. That was it. Nothing more.

The day passed. The sun set. The skies opened up as the stars moved in. Day turned into night.

The stars were familiar to me now. I had known them all my life but was just now seeing them. They were not so much a pattern in the night sky, Instead they were a part of me. They were points of me that extended beyond the confines of my skin.

I knew we had always been connected. It just took me some time to realize how deeply.

It was with that familiarity that I crawled into the sheets of my bed that evening. They were homespun and wonderfully rough with the rawness of cotton. They were cool and solid and real. Real without the refinement of factory processing or softeners. Real with the smell of the island from being hung on a line all day. Real with the smells of olive trees and grapevines, of that reddish soil from the earth and the salt from the sea.

I drifted off to sleep that night anticipating the boat and the man I knew without knowing.

THIRD NIGHT

The Human Experience

The third night began like all the others. There was a shift somewhere in my consciousness that I was not aware of. At some point after nestling into the quiet of my mind I rose on the other side of the looking glass to find myself on our little boat.

He was already there, sitting across from me. His thoughts were already there as if in a cloud that hovered around him. I wandered into it without moving. I simply became aware of our conversation just as I became aware of myself in that moment.

His thoughts resonated through me. The ideas that he felt I felt. The emotions that he lived in I lived in. I almost smiled at the way in which our thoughts were woven together. The duality of our ideas resonated as questions formed in my mind.

Around me the boat, the sea, the stars all seemed more real in so many ways than they ever had when I was awake. It was as if I saw each from multiple points of view at once. At that moment I knew I was no longer dreaming. I was experiencing.

My mind reeled with the thought of what is and is not, what was a dream and what was reality. How both were two sides of the same coin. How one could not exist without the other and how we were in an eternal drift, back and forth between the two. Our consciousness was the thread that connected the two through the ebb and flow of existence, free from borders and hard lines.

"It is a wonderful mechanism is it not?" he said.

"At times it is like a celestial clock with gears and cogs all meshing in synchronicity. At other times it is like the sea itself where everything simply flows in the endless tide of existence."

That thought calmed me. It focused my mind on the visuals for what was rather than on the endless possibilities of what could be.

"The human experience are nothing but a lens through which you perceive the energy that is. Your greatest minds have told you this for eons. "I think therefore I am." Yet you continue to place your hands on the table before you and say "I feel this. This is real. Therefore I am real too."

He seemed to smile in a far off way. It was a smile that I followed to the horizon and back again. I felt the wood of the railing and dipped my hand over the side to feel the cool wetness of the water. The water shimmered in the moonlight as it slipped back into the sea that was all around us.

"It is not, you know," was all he said. "It is merely your perception of what actually is. The Love you have within you is what opens the world up to you. There is more empty space between the atoms of that water than there are solid particles on the planet it sits on. What holds them together is simply energy.

"The same is true of the home you live in. There is less solid matter in the entire structure of a house than there is space between. What little matter that exists is held together with energy. It is not the wood of the house that you feel. It is the energy that connects it all together that you feel. There is no magic to this. It is science and faith and truth. Nothing more."

He smiled to me in a kind and knowing way.

"The atoms themselves are nothing more than a reflection of the possibilities for what can be. Inside each atom are infinitely small strands of energy. Each takes shape through your senses based on your mind's best guess for where they are and what they should be.

"Yours is a world of uncertainty. It is a world of not knowing for sure of what is and what is not. Some view the world through the lens of hat and anger. Others through the lens of Love. Which lens you see the world through is for you to discover and decide.

"Your most respected minds understand probability over reality. They apply their best guess on an object's position. This is based on probabilities and logic as to an object's location in space and time. Even they acknowledge it is, in that final millisecond, an assumption based on the laws they created to explain the actions of the Universe.

"Theirs is an effort to make sense of the physical world they witness before stepping into the metaphysical. The same is true of you. That little string of energy exists within each of you, but is only drawn to life as your consciousness touches upon it. It is that connection that gives your world form and substance.

"The real question is not what is, but what you are aware of. The deck of this boat is nothing. Until you are aware of it. The energy that runs throughout the deck is the same as that runs through you. It simply lacks consciousness. It is why you can so easily find attachment to a stone or a tree or a piece of furniture. It is your consciousness that brings it into being. It is that consciousness which ties it all together."

"That thread of consciousness defies space and time. It is a constant. It is the energy of Love.

"When in doubt, always look for the threads throughout your journey. Those threads can be woven together to create a tapestry that points the way, and illuminates the truth that lies beneath all things."

"Seek out the patterns of nature. Within them lies the answers you seek. They have provided the answer for eons.

"In so many ways God has been described as omnipotent and everlasting, the Alpha and the Omega. God is no different than the energy of Love, an underlying force that has always been and always will be.

"God and Love, by any other name, is the connector that guides how everything interacts on the micro and macro levels. The energy of both defy space and time to define the underlying actions of every atom in existence. Do you see that God is Love? They are one and the same.

"There is no right or wrong answers to Love or to God. They are simply words for the same idea. The idea of understanding what already is. We travel along our paths and witness the patterns. We try to make sense of them and learn through that effort. In the end, existence is what it is. It is we who change our perspective to match what is already there.

"At some point it is up to each of us to look around, to see what is truly there, free from judgment so that we can acknowledge the simple truth to what is and has always been. In the end of our journeys, each of us returns to the beginning with a new perspective of what can be."

I knew what he was talking about. A thread of energy that transcended space and time. That connected all things and linked my actions to those around me. I have seen my actions create a wave that others became a part of. That wave rebounded off of other events and rejoined me later in life.

"Is this Karma?" I asked.

"Karma is one way to describe a very fundamental rule of existence. *The Conservation of Energy* is another. The idea that energy cannot be created or destroyed. It can only change form one form to another. Just like the words God and Love, these are different words for the same idea.

"The energy of your actions from one day follow you to the next. 'What goes around, comes around,' as you might say. All point to the same outcome, that you are simply an echo of your consciousness. Your energy is always there, connection you through what you see as reality. What you do in one life follows you to the next because your true energy is alive in the flow of the Love that is all around your true self. Not in your body.

"The energy of your thoughts and actions does not fade with the sun. The energy that you garner stays with you throughout your life. There is no mysterious force that follows you from here to there. It is all simply you.

"What you forget is that you are far greater than the physical self that you see. Every thought you have, every action you take is more a part of you than your physical self. You may live in the physical world, but your being reaches far beyond.

"The energy you carry is more you than the physical outline of your body. It is up to you to recognize this if you are to bring the two together.

"Every thought and every action you take sets off a cascade of events. Just as when a pebble drops into the ocean its ripples reach out. When you show Love to someone, the energy of your actions do the same. It ripples outward so that others can feel it.

"The ripples on the surface are just one part of what occurs. This is the visible effect of your actions on the people closest t you. But beneath the surface your actions reverberate throughout the existence. Every ripple that extends from you adds to the waves and wavelets that are.

"There are many words to describe how your energy acts and reacts to the energy around you. Each echoes a very simple concept that is at the core of existence. That is why it is so hard to comprehend, not for its complexity, but for its vastness."

"Like so many other words, Karma has lost its meaning. It is a word that has been used for centuries to explain the current of energy that flows beneath everything. Karma describes the fact that there is one energy that is the source of all energy.

"The threads of Karma exists beyond time and space. It is a constant as you change from one form to the next and from one life to another. It transcends the physics of the physical. It is an acknowledgement that everything is connected after the mind can no longer comprehend what is beyond the walls of logic.

"That thread of energy connects every action from the past and future to the present. It creates a cascade that may seem to take on a life of its own. In the end Karma is simply a word for the energy that connects everything through the physical, mental and spiritual states of being.

"It is proof that physics and metaphysics are one. Each follows the same rules of existence, and at the core of each is the energy of Love.

"The more Love that is allowed to build within an action, the more powerful and positive that action becomes. When the Love within an event becomes so great that it cannot contain itself, it overflows the banks of the river that contains it.

When that happens the Love that is overflows the banks of time and place. It creates a thread that lasts through eternity. That thread, that Karma, is the current of energy that a spirit creates as it travels on their journey through time and space, through existence."

"What happens to that thread when two people are in Love?"

"Look to nature. When two spirits come together in a Love that is pure, it is as if two streams join to create a river. Their energy combines to break through the banks that once confined them. Each overflows its banks to surge into the ocean beyond. Together they create a new current and a new point of consciousness.

"The original Love is still there. It simply takes on a new and wonderful form with more layers and deeper currents than ever before. The pure Love of two people is not limited to their bodies. It grows to the limits of existence. It expands to create a new point of consciousness to engulf those who are open to their growing energy.

"The expanding Love that is, is reflected in the idea of a family, of a tribe, of friends. It is shared over time and space. A true family is only limited by the Love of those within it. Not by the laws of society. Not by the ideals of a single person. Laws change based on human need. Love remains as Love no matter who finds it.

"To truly appreciate the energy of Love you must think beyond the physical and understand the connections that Love creates within your being at every level.

Jeff Cannon

"When you open up to Love, you begin to understand the unlimited potential it provides. You begin to understand the limitlessness of yourself within all of existence."

"So we can be more than a single point of consciousness."

"Love is not about how big, but how pure. No matter what size or form the vessel takes the Love within it is the same. The Love you feel may be on a different scale than the Love of all existence but it is still there. You may see it from a different perspective. You may experience it in different ways, but in the end it is the same. Just as drops of water may come from different sources, once they enter the ocean those differences disappear. Those drops become the ocean.

"It is the essence of all creation. There is no difference between the Love we all swim in and the Love two people feel for each other. The affection a person feels for an animal or a plant or a work of art all comes from the same energy. Each is simply a different current flowing on its own path, expressed in a different way and on a different scale.

"When a family or a tribe becomes too concerned with the physical makeup of its members, it begins to lose the Love

122

beneath it. Some members spin off to search out a new family and to return to the Love that was.

"It is no different in the sea of Love. Everything is eternally in a constant state of flow. Beneath this is the energy of Love. The human experience is simply an echo of that reality.

"When two people join together in Love, truly in Love, there is so much more than just a physical bond. There is a spiritual bond that echoes across the universe and all existence as well. That is the Love that will heal voids and the fabric of existence.

"It is why the act of making Love can be as much a spiritual act as a physical one. The act of coupling two bodies is not spiritual in and of itself. It becomes spiritual when you join your awareness with the divinity that is in all things.

"The point where you truly experience the Love in each other is the point where the connection you create flows openly and without boundaries. It becomes spiritual because you are opening yourself to the divine that is in you.

"Some cultures view the act of sex as a sacred act. They do so not because the physical act brings you closer to the divine but because the act of two people uniting in their Love mirrors the greater journey we are all on. When you open yourself to the divine it makes you distinctly aware of the divinity in all things."

"That very realization is why you feel such betrayal and such loss when you lose Love. The space where Love once flowed so freely is now empty. In its place is a window into the void that each is trying to heal.

"Your very physical brain tries to fill that void with the only thing it knows to be so bleak; the feelings of betrayal and anger, fear and doubt. It is not just the loss of Love that hurts. It is the realization of the emptiness that awaits.

"When you lose Love you begin to comprehend the vastness and the emptiness of the abyss. You begin to understand the depth to which the void can extend. That is a horrible concept to understand. Even if it lasts for but a fraction of a moment on the scale of timelessness it is forever burned into your being.

"Put your hand into the ocean and push the water away. That space is empty for the briefest of moments. The water surrounding your hand rushes back in t fill it instantly.

The void is filled the same way. The void can be filled almost before it is emptied. But you will forever remember that moment of nothingness.

"It is not that Love is no longer. It is that you have seen into that void and recognized the unbearable darkness within it."

"Is that were hate and anger and fear come from?"

"When a baby is born it is born with Love and kindness. There is nothing else. Infants do not try to harm each other over riches or land. They do not steal food out of the mouths of their brothers and sisters. They do not act out of jealousy. They do not hate. They help each other.

"They simply respond to the world around them. They simply want to experience existence through the filter of the human experience. They squirm and shift as they try to establish themselves in their new form.

"They learn to protect the fragile body they were given. They cry when they sense they need food. They smile when they learn something new. They open their eyes and stare when they want to connect with another. They laugh when they find Love. They learn the emotions of the human form as they grow.

"Pain, fear and anger are not bad emotions. They are simply the body's way of telling them something is wrong. That there is a void before them. It is just the way every human body translates the nothingness of the world into a language your very

physical self can understand.

"It is sad. But it is the way in which you learn. It follows the

patterns of all existence. Existence does not have books to read

or schools to attend, it flows from one experience to the next.

With each experience your consciousness expands as you learn

to become one with what already is."

At that moment the boat, the water, even the star-filled sky

disappeared to me as my attention grew to envelope what was

right before me. It was filled with the meaning behind his words.

With a greater level of awareness.

"Then what about bigotry?" I asked?

"Bigotry is not an emotion to the world around you. It is

taught. It is learned out of hate and fear. It is a complex process

that wraps emotions with the teachings of someone already deep

in their own void. Bigotry twists the fabric of life into a lie.

"What many people forget is that if someone can learn

bigotry they can also learn Love. The mind and body learns to

respond to the world and the events around them. Many

responses are learned as a way to live together in harmony. Others are learned to avoid pain.

"Positive responses are based on giving and helping, forgiving and caring, compassion and equanimity. They echo the ebb and flow of existence. They help each understand the flow of Love and of community.

"Responses like bigotry are taught in the opposite way. They come from weak minds filled with fear. They are not a sign of strength, but just the opposite. The emotions that a young mind uses to avoid danger can overwhelm those that seek Love and growth. They are learned from those not strong enough to look within and recognize the inherent Love and beauty that is there.

"Those who preach the words of hate and fear are aware of the void that is before everyone. They are so afraid of what they see that they are paralyzed into inaction. They learn to be more comfortable with the lack of energy flowing through them than with the endless possibilities that Love brings. The void expands within them. They in turn cower into their own darkness.

"Their life becomes a self-fulfilling prophesy of emptiness, fear and anger. They would rather experience emptiness than seek balance in the energy that is all around them.

"In the end theirs is an experience that is to be repeated over and over again until they learn to stop and face the fears that have trapped them. Those unable to bring Love into their existence are weighted down with layers of darkness. Each layer is formed by the perception that there is a lack of existence. Each reflects the cold emptiness of the void, of being without Love."

"Those who live in darkness are unwilling to see the path that is right before them. Each step is taken with fear that there will be no ground for their foot to touch upon. They shrink within themselves and move further from the Love and light that is all around them. They are so focused on the void that they cannot see the beauty of existence that is right all around them.

"This is a part of the journey. It is a part of the human experience. They have simply chosen to take a longer route to the inevitable. Even bigotry will purify their being in the end. It is the inevitability of the human experience. It may take several lifetimes, but in the end even they will eventually find Love.

"What is more important than the emptiness is what comes from the fullness that will inevitably be. Regardless of what someone experiences in a single life they will find that it is always possible to return to Love by simply giving Love.

"That knowledge is the inevitability of the experience. Beneath every human is awash in the sea of Love. No matter where you find yourself, deep within you there is always Love.

"It starts with the smallest of gestures. Perhaps it is a smile. Perhaps it is a Loving thought. Each opens a door that allows more energy to flow in. Each sends a thread across the void upon which an entire bridge can be built. The cycle of Love begins to spin, weaving a tapestry upon which even more Love can pass.

"Once begun it is simply a matter of staying open and not blocking the energy that is already coming through. Just like the water filling a void, the Love within will flow."

"Love, empathy and compassion are universal truths. Of these, Love is the truth of existence. It takes the smallest of efforts to rejoin current that is all around each of us. Remove the layers that life creates and you remove the walls that prevent the energy of existence from flowing freely.

"To you that means giving time, and time is not something you are very good with. Just know that the Love you seek will always be there. You can find it at any time. You just have to remain open to it."

I turned from him to watch our wake. It was speckled with green luminescence. It was the track of our boat from all of the tiny creatures we had disturbed by our passage. It was their shock at being touched that illuminated their bioluminescence. Was that fear or anger? Was it Love? Or was it simply their energy responding to ours as we touched?

I felt glad at their signal. I felt sad that we could not say more.

"Why is war and aggression such a part of human nature?"

"Aggression does no leads to fights or wars. They are started by fear. The first fight was started by two humans before they even knew they were human. They were two creatures, scared and hungry. They saw the void and in that moment they saw the finality of what could be.

"One wanted to feel whole but did not know how to ask. The other knew that Love existed but did not know how to open to it. They only knew that there was good and that they were without.

"They were too afraid to reach out to each other for help. Unwilling to open their arms they threw rocks and ran away.

Again and again they reached out. Again and again they ran away.

"Each time they ran, they found themselves alone, not realizing just how alone they were. They each wanted Love, but they did not know how to ask for it. They did not know that all they had to do to receive Love was to give Love.

"There is no way to know how many millennia they continued to fight and run. Inevitably one of them stopped and opened its arms, trusting the other to do the same."

"At one point human nature changed. Human nature changed the same way the nature of any animal in the wild changes. Through trial and error and experience. What is it you say? 'The definition of insanity is doing the same thing over and over again and expecting a different result?'

"Seeing how nothing changed, one reached out with empathy to the other. In time they survived, not by being alone but by being together. The stronger one realized that no matter how strong they were they were weak without the Love of the other. They needed the support and the Love if they were to be something more than what they were already.

"In that moment humanity blossomed. The human experience was no longer about surviving but about flourishing. It is the growth that can only happen when there is Love."

"This pattern occurs again and again throughout all of existence. Each time a spirit remains open to the circuit of Love it realizes the enormity of its potential. That knowledge makes it easier to remain open. Every time it becomes easier to keep from blocking the flow evolve and to flourish.

"It is that first step that is the most difficult. It is that first moment of trust that is the hardest to open up to. Yet it is inevitable. Every time two people come together it starts slowly. Each time it gets easier to trust and to remain open. Each time fear plays a smaller role. It is time that is the question in the human experience, not the inevitability of the outcome. In time, you will find Love, it is inevitable."

"The first war was started the same way as the first conflict. There were two tribes. One tribe was scared and hungry. The other had what crops they were able to pull from the earth. The first wanted what the other had.

"They attacked not from strength but from fear. The fear of being turned away if they asked for help. The fear of being turned away was stronger than their hope for Love. It was easier for them to hit than to ask.

"In time both tribes survived. It was not because one overpowered the other. It was because they realized that they were stronger through Love than through hate. It was with their ability to work together that they survived.

"Throughout time it is the wars that stand out in history. Just as the void stands out for its darkness. But it is the healing that comes after that has fueled the growth of humanity, and where humanity has blossomed.

"Every battle that has ever occurred only stalled the inevitable. When those battles were forgotten the Love and compassion that has always brought humans together blooms. Compassion and understanding has always been the true sign of strength. It is Love that has always helped people overcome. It is Love and compassion that have enabled every spirit to achieve greatness in the balance they seek."

Those words reverberated through my head. It was difficult to look anywhere and not see the balance. It started with our little craft. The sail pushed by the wind and balanced against the keel beneath the waves that drove us forward. The hull rested between the two in the rise and fall of the sea. Even the dark water balanced against the sky with the horizon. Everywhere I looked I saw it.

"If it is about Love, then why don't we naturally follow the path of Love?" I asked.

"You do. With every step you take, your journey continues. If each step was the right one there would be no journey. It is why the wrong steps are just as important as the right ones. The path you travel is what is important. Not your destination.

"Inevitably you will end right where you are meant to be. You will learn the lessons and experience existence through the shell of humanity. You might not take the shortest path, but that is okay. Every path will get you where you need to go in the end.

"You are inquisitive because you are here to learn. The process for learning is accomplished by questioning. The more you question the more you wander from the path. The more you wander the more you learn how to return to your path. That is the nature of existence.

"Over and over again this pattern repeats itself. If you watch a stream after a rain, it does not know where to flow. It trickles down until it finds its path. The same is true for you.

Throughout all of humanity people have questioned in search of answers. At times people created false answers to avoid the change they feared. But that never stopped people from questioning. Inevitably truth has a way of rising to the top. It follows Love. Which is a lesson in itself. It is just a matter of time before you eventually become your path."

"The beautiful classroom of existence is that it can be seen through the patterns it creates. To find the truth within simply observe what is around you. When you seek answers in the natural order of the Universe the truth is there waiting for you.

"Every time humans find truth they advance and evolve; for behind every truth is the energy of Love. Love leads to growth. Fear leads to stagnation."

"Every time you seek answers with truth you begin a new journey. The destination of any journey is never the answer you first sought. The more you learn the more your question changes. You revise it based on your new sense of self. Your destination does not change, it is only modified by the new boundaries you establish.

"There is an inherent need for all beings to explore their boundaries. It is our way to understand the vantage point from which we observe all things.

"If you truly want answers you must first overcome your own ego, your own fear, your own human nature. You must overcome the limits of your physical and mental self. Only then will you come upon the answer and the growth you seek."

Looking past myself and my friend I understood the balance in his wisdom. It was the balance of the universe. I could see it within him and around him. I could see it on a scale, larger than I had ever imagined before. I was only reminded by the touch of the tiller about the realities of life in the physical world.

"How does this relate to the killing and violence we see?"

"Where two planes meet, there is always turbulence. The balance of the physical and the metaphysical is that point right now for the human experience.

"When the answers sought do not fit the desires behind the questions, fear is the result. The body says 'stop, let us be safe.' The mind says 'but we are not yet at our destination.' The body says 'this is far enough. It will do just fine.' The mind says, 'but there is so much more'

"Between the body and the mind, between the physical and the metaphysical is the human experience. People fear the unknown. It reflects the void that is created between the two planes. It is not without. It is within.

"Rather than explore that which makes them uncomfortable, people try to stop whatever it is that is causing them pain. If only they stepped off of their path and questioned their pain, to look at the source of their fear they would find it within themselves.

"All people seek to protect themselves. They want to stay where they are safe. They would rather stagnate where they are and try to stop the inevitable than to explore the boundless opportunities that are everywhere.

"It takes energy to rise above the physical. But that is what you must do in order to seek the spiritual. It takes a lot to look past the ego and the fear that has rooted itself so deeply. But that is what must be done if you are to acknowledge the Love that is all around. That is the process of enlightenment.

"As with everything in existence, the inevitability of enlightenment creates the way. In the end you will learn the lessons you need to rise above. It is just a matter of how many layers you must go through before uncovering the ones that can be cast aside."

"Just know that humans have never survived by killing each other. Killing and war have only slowed the process before those fighting discover what they already knew - that no man or woman is an island. That survival is based on Love, not ego or fear or anger or hate.

"Humans, as all things, are an echo of the consciousness that floats in the sea of Love. They in turn survive by loving each other. They continue to survive by helping each other and by giving up their own egos and interests, sacrificing themselves for each other. It is only through giving that receiving is possible.

"In their hearts every person knows this. Unfortunately not every person acknowledges this. Once that is realized it is easy to step beyond the human experience and into the larger pool of existence. The human experience is a way for the consciousness to witness the sea of existence through a different lens. It is a step toward the inevitable enlightenment we will all attain.

"Sometimes it is easier to think of the human experience as a playground within which to learn, free from the potential for being harmed. You are here to experience existence and Love, through the filters of humanity. You will learn each lesson you need to learn. In the end you will remove the barriers that now prevent you from evolving to your own divinity.

"This is the process of enlightenment and of transcendence. You learn a lesson. A layer drops away. You grow lighter. You rise above. At different points you step back to relearn what you already know before you realize that you knew it all along.

"In time you will learn to apply a lesson that you learned over there to a question that arose over here so that you can polish off a burr that exists on your consciousness.

"Evolution is an inevitability. The path you choose to take there is the choice you have in life and is reflected in every layer of your own existence."

"Just know that throughout life there are instances of great pain and suffering. There have always been instances of great pain and suffering throughout humanity and across the world. There have been times when humans have pushed their own survival to the brink of extinction. Yet, they have always pulled back.

"This is a pattern that has repeated itself since humanity began. It is a pattern that will continue to repeat itself well into the future. Each time the human collective learns a lesson it moves forward together. When an individual learns a lesson, that one person inches the collective forward.

"Every time people grow they do so by moving beyond themselves. They overcome their individual needs and think beyond their own individuality. They turn to their true nature, that of Love. That is where true power lies.

"This is true of friendships. This is true of marriage and relationships. This is true for corporations and entire countries. This is the nature of the Universe. It is the truth of Love. Love cannot be destroyed. It is all around you. It can only change form based on your needs and the needs of humanity as a whole."

"When you return to the purity of yourself, you do not act out of ego but out of the interest of the greater good. For the best interest for humanity is also your best interest. Each is a reflection of the Love we all swim in.

"When you act out of Love you notice a change in your own energy. You notice a wall has come down. You realize a door has opened. You notice that life has become easier and happier. You notice that you are filled with more Love than when you started.

"When you see violence in the world. You feel sad. You feel ashamed that people can treat other people this way. Hope fades. A door closes. It is a lesson for you.

"When you feel violence within yourself you feel the same way. You know that you have not acted out of purity. You feel guilt. Hope fades. A door closes."

"When a feeling of darkness overcomes you. It frightens you. It makes you want to return to the Love you know is within you. If you cannot find the Love you want you become angry and ever more frightened. You feel yourself return to the primal muck from which you grew.

"You know the way to go but you are unable to rise above your own ego to find what you sense is inside. Now you have a choice. Do you return to the false safety of the physical, or do you rise above and seek to transcend?

"Throughout all of humanity returning to the primal has always been the easy solution. Finding the strength to see the path ahead and having the strength to follow that path has always been the question. Following is the more difficult task, but its rewards are far richer than the risks it poses.

"As humanity evolves and grows toward its own divinity the way becomes clearer. It is why there are far more souls seeking than at the dawn of humanity. Your journey is not simply to find an answer to your question. It is to gain a new perspective from which to grow. It is to look into your own divinity and to realize it is closer now than ever before."

And here we were again. The old ideas of balance and perspective, of Ying and Yang, of ebb and flow, of that never-ending movement through which we must pass if we are to evolve. There was a path. It was there all along, but for the first time it was more clearly defined for me.

His words did more than ring true. They spoke to the thread reflected in the changing social mores of the world cultures. Not in the rules intended to tear people apart, but in the connections that brought people together across disparate places and cultures.

Inside I screamed that life was a beautiful thing, that people were good, and that our divinity was not an aberration saved for just a few, but a part of the natural order to nature itself.

"What happens to all of this when we die?"

"When you see death you are too close to the circle of life. Death is perception. Not reality. Love is the reality. You know it is there. Death is merely how you perceive that moment when someone's energy is set free from the human experience.

"What you call life is but a small arc on the larger circle. You are born, you live, and you die is simply a small segment of a much larger circle that repeats itself over and over again in many forms.

"When the human body stops functioning the energy within is released from the physical form. That energy simply does what all energy does. It flows past the boundaries of humanity. It returns to the sea of energy to become one again.

"When one person's energy passes from one life to another the shell they occupied is left behind. They are free from the limitations that once isolated them. Their energy is released into the pool of Love that is all around us.

"It is the same as if the walls of a water droplet were released. The water inside is free to join the sea it is now a part of. It becomes a part of the constant ebb and flow as its energy is released to find its own balance. The energy that is released fuels the currents of the universe and of existence. What is left behind is an empty shell to be returned to the physical world it came from. What was inside transcends the human experience to become more whole than it ever was, now more complete with the lessons of the human experience your true self has gained.

"This is the difference between the surface ripple seen when a drop strikes the ocean and the ripples that reverberate beneath. The essence of you remains unique. It is the impact of your experience that is felt forever.

"When you enter the sea you are no longer alone. You bring the energy of your experience with you. Your energy changes the composition of the entire sea, even if that difference is imperceptible. It may be impossible to see where the drop ends and the ocean begins, but it is there.

"That is the duality of existence. You return to being a concentration of Love in the sea of existence. You return to being part of the endless waves and tides that are. The rhythms of your spirit reflect your consciousness that is you. You return to where you were, now slightly different and with a new perspective."

"Remember, the Universe and everything around you is nothing but energy. Every bump you see, every snowflake you watch, every ocean you float upon is simply your way of translating the energy into a form that is compatible with your humanity. Every memory you experience is how you see the concentration of energy that has flowed through you.

"Every snowflake always lands perfectly. You mark it with a date and time to make sense of it in the human experience. What you think you see, hear, taste and feel is just your body's way of making sense out of the energy that is the event you witnessed.

"How you realize the energy that is around you is unique to you. It is to everyone. The reality you create for yourself is slightly different from the reality of everyone else. The experience you think you are enjoying is unique to you. It is for everyone. That is why two people can look at the same event and see two different things. It is the difference between perception and reality. Perception you see to be true. Reality is true, even though you may not recognize it a such.

"So am I not here, in this dream?" I asked.

"Oh, you are here," he replied. "You are very much here. You are also in your bed renewing your body. Each is a reflection of your true self. Each is a lens through which you interact with the energy that is. Each provides you with a different vantage point from which to witness existence; body, mind, and spirit.

"Just as there are many different facets to your personality, there are many different facets to the energy that is you. Each is a prism with which to experience the energy that is all around you, that is within you. None is more true or less false than another; they are simply different sides of your complete self. Merge them into one and you become whole."

"How you perceive yourself is how you allow your humanity to define you. It is not real. The reality is that all of existence awaits your energy. Let go of the shell of humanity, and the doors of eternity open.

"Beneath it all you are a concentration of Love. The Love that glows within you is no less than the Love that glows at the center of a star.

146

"You have taken a form that is different than that of a star, but at your core your energy burns just the same. You are and always will be a concentration of Love, a concentration that birthed your consciousness into being. Your consciousness provides you with a level of awareness that is what makes you unique. Just like a raindrop or a snowflake, there is not another entity anywhere in existence like you. Out there, there is an entire ocean waiting for you to join when you are ready."

"It is beautiful," I said.

"It is," he agreed.

"When your consciousness was sparked into existence, it reverberated no less than the Big Bang, or when God uttered the words 'Let There Be Light.' At that moment you began your journey of refinement. You spun your consciousness this way and that, forever polishing your energy to fit within the energy that is all around you. It is a process all things go through. You removed the rough spots to free yourself of the voids and the gaps that exist between each point of consciousness. Those voids are neither good or bad. They are simply the spaces left from your moment of conception.

"Each of us have taken on many experiences and many skins through which to explore our truths. After each experience we return to the sea in a purer state than when we left."

"It is the human experience that enables us to witness the Love of Existence without being consumed by it. If you witnessed it in its raw state of being it would blind you, sending you back to your point of creation. The very senses that limit you as a human also provide the buffer you need to explore all that is.

"It is the human experience that is the filter between you and the reality of existence. The senses that you feel and the thoughts that you have are a very human response to what your consciousness witnesses as it grows and expands.

"Think of the awe within your mind as you witness something you have never witnessed before. Now think of that feeling on a scale you cannot even begin to imagine.

"You experience the Love that is all around you. Only you do so in increments through sight and sound, smell and taste, touch and yes, with your heart. Each provides you with a small window toward the inevitable; that of recognizing the full consciousness that is you, free from any limits.

"As your awareness grows your true energy deepens. Only when you are free will you understand the depth of the Love that is within your true self. When you are free of the human experience you will flow beyond the walls of humanity to touch everything that is, free of time or space. But it is only through the human experience that you learn to do so.

"As your consciousness expands you will learn to manage the Love that is all around you, that is within you. You will learn to grow comfortable with the lack of boundaries until you become one again.

"As your awareness transcends the five senses you will become aware of a sixth sense, of a seventh, an eighth and an infinite number more. You will become aware of awareness itself that would leave you gasping for recognition if you witnessed it now.

"Look around. Right now you are aware of people with greater insight than you. You are also aware of energies and sensations that others are unable to perceive. In so many ways you already transcend the human body that you once thought was all there was of you.

"With each experience, with each life, you grow less reliant on your form. You become more radiant. As your radiance

149

grows the distance between you and the ocean of Love lessens. You grow enlightened.

"Each step toward enlightenment removes the boundary that once defined the drop that was you. The more you discover the sea of Love the more you become a part of the Love that is. As you do the Universe that you thought was everything disappears.

"That is the moment of transcendence. When you pass on you do not travel to a new place. You become aware of the place you are already in and you see the endless nature of the Love that has always been all around you."

"You will become aware that the energy which runs through you is the single thread of connection between our worlds. It is the thread that connects you with all things. The rocks, the trees, the birds, the very energy that is at the core of your being is woven with all of the energies of existence."

"When you witness it in its entirety you will laugh at its simplicity. It is in your experience right here and now. It is in your sleeping body. It is in your work and your play. It is in your consciousness and the collective consciousness that is shared by all of humanity.

"Your energy is a part of the greater pool of energy that is. What makes you unique is that you are aware of your individuality and of yourself. It is your sense of self that echoes through all eternity. It is your consciousness and sense of self upon which the waves reverberate.

"Like a drop of water in the ocean, the more you grow aware of the boundaries that once defined you, the less you are aware of the sea that is all around you. The balance you seek is found in the limitlessness of full awareness while still being aware of that which is you. That is the duality between you and the endless eternity of existence. The finite and the infinite.

"The moment you recognize this is the moment you become whole and present with creation.

"The boundaries that separate you from that moment are the boundaries that define your consciousness. Let go of those boundaries and you let go of the walls that keep you from the beauty of everything that is."

"The knowledge of being human keeps you apart from all that is. It is in the safety of the human experience that allows you to explore what it is to be divine.

"That is your journey. That is everyone's journey. That is the journey of existence. It is to remove the barriers that prevent the energy from flowing around you and through you. When it does, when you are nothing, you become everything.

"That is your moment of truth. It is the moment that each of your experiences moves you forward, the moment when your truth mirrors the truth of all existence because you are existence.

"It is the many enlightenments on your journey that will carry you past being and into Love. Your journey takes you from where you are, to where you are. But, it gives you a new vantage point from which to understand all of creation."

He painted an image for me of travel to nowhere and to everywhere. It is a journey about energy, where waves glisten with the reflection of our consciousness, of our true self.

"What happens when there is nothing but pure Love left? What happens when there are no voids to fill?"

"Let there be light?" was all he said with a glimmer that left me in awe and wonder.

"The moment all of the points of consciousness that are come together, it is for an eternity that lasts the briefest of moments. It is an incomprehensible flash of creation that begins the largest cycle all over again. It is a moment that flows from one dream to the next. It is the moment of recognition when you realize you are in the middle of a thought while meditating on an unimaginable scale.

"You cannot define that moment. It is beyond comprehension. You can ask yourself, 'how long did the Big Bang last?' How long was each of the six days that He worked before He rested? How long did the Raven fly before dropping its seed into the sea from which sprang he lands of the earth?

"And that was just for one universe. This is for all of existence. What came before it? How long does a moment of no existence exist when there was no time and space for it to exist in?

"It existed in its non-existence. In a moment of pure consciousness."

"In that point of non-existence there is still Love. For it cannot be destroyed. It is the pool of water in which the lotus flower blossomed anew. A new existence is created out of the energy of the old. One does not die to start another. One simply fades from being and another flows into the emptiness left behind. The seeds of new universes are once again strewn across existence and consciousness takes shape on a new plane.

"Step further back than you can imagine. Think of all you have ever experienced. Now let it go. Allow your mind's eye to see existence as every moment you have never dreamed of.

"Now see all of those experiences as tiny dots from across the universe. Imagine all those dots from every point of view as stars and realize that there are as many stars in the Milky Way as there are cells in a single brain. There are as many galaxies in the universe as there are connections between those cells.

"See that and you begin to see the scale upon which you are asking. There are infinite universes. Each universe is a flower that blossoms in a pond filled with flowers. Each flower sends its seeds into the air once it has bloomed to create new flowers on a cosmic level unimagined.

"There is no finite *why*. There simply *is* and *is* is endless. "

"Through all of this your journey is not taken with the steps of a giant. It is taken with tiny steps of refinement. It is less about reaching a destination as it is discovering a new beginning that you are traveling toward. Polish the rough edges left from the fires of creation and you will fit into the bliss of eternity, free from the voids that prevent energy from passing.

"This cycle repeats itself in every atom of existence. The closer you come to being a pure body free from voids, the smaller is the distance you must travel but the greater are the details to focus upon.

"The first step is largest. It is the hardest to take. The final steps are the smallest. They are also the most difficult. The closer you get, the longer the journey becomes, but the more joy you will find in the experience. The less doubt you carry, the higher you can fly and the freer you can soar.

"At such a point there is less searching and more understanding. Your consciousness melts into the consciousness of everything. You are no longer limited by time and space. There is no fear. There is no hesitation. There is simply the energy that flows within and without, back and forth in the endless currents of Love.

"You may understand that moment but I doubt you can comprehend it. It is a moment in eternity when you are everything and nothing. When you are both mother and child, creator and being."

"Touch upon this lightly. Do not hold it too close. To try to understand eternity now is to be a child who dreams of being an adult. There are so many nuances that maturity will remain a dream until you are in the midst of the changes to come. And yes, that too is part of the human experience.

"When you were a child you envied the idea of being an adult, but your mind could only think as a child. You were unaware of the nuances that come with age and experience. Without knowing the right questions to ask you were not able to learn the answers until you experienced it for yourself. Only when you understood the questions could you understand the answers. By that time, you no longer needed to ask.

"With each new answer you learned another question and the cycle began again. You created a momentary calm for yourself as if a giant hand pushed aside the water of existence, opening the way for the energies of Love to rush in and fill the void. In that event a new reality was created for you to experience.

"Like a dream, or a tide, it is a never ending cycle without beginning or end."

I looked out at the sea. It reflected the stars in the sky on the smooth waves. Without a horizon to separate the two the sky and the sea blended together. Separate but one.

"But why? If existence never ceases and we just keep changing form to experience Love from a new perspective, what is the purpose?"

"Why is a beautiful question."

He seemed to nod. Perhaps even to ponder.

"Why not? Is the obvious answer," he said with a smile.

"But that is never enough is it?

"You are looking for a finite answer to an infinite question. You have a limited mind boxed in by the thought of a destination that is already in your mind.

"Existence is not a destination. It is a journey. It is not a place. It is a state of mind. It is energy. When you think of a place you limit your ability to comprehend that existence is infinite. Only in your immeasurable expanse is it finite.

"The goal is not to reach a point of arrival. It is to understand the finite within the infinite. There is no finish line to cross. There is simply the eternal ebb and flow of energy that washes over you and through you. To understand that is all that is."

"And where do I find that in nature?" I asked my own mind.

"It is all around you." He replied without moving his lips.

"Have you ever wondered why you can lose yourself watching the waves as they crash upon the shore? Have you ever wondered why the gentle rocking of a boat so easily lulls you to sleep? Are you not the least bit curious as to why you so eagerly await another Autumn?

"Existence is the calm found in all things. When you understand the endless nature of existence, you understand the limits within the question of 'why?'"

"In time you will find some questions are simply too large and too interwoven to comprehend at this level. In time you will discover that the simplest answers are most often the right ones.

Sometimes simply being is enough. Sometimes learning how to be is the journey and the destination at the same time.

"It is when you have asked all the complex questions that you will return to the simplest. The moment you are able to understand the answers you no longer need the questions."

"A clock. A sea. Is there a simple way to describe how it all works?" That was what my mind put together.

"Simple, yes. Complete?" He seemed to laugh. "That depends on your perspective.

"You must understand that there is infinite energy in existence. That energy comes together and dissipates in a never ending ebb and flow. It is a tide beyond comprehension. It spans universes and time. Within that tide there are points of consciousness. Each point creates its own reality based on its perspective. That perspective is about far more than just sight. It is an experience.

"The energy of existence, the Love that is, forever changes on a scale that is larger and deeper than you could ever conceive. It is echoed in the energy of the Universe. It forever comes together, splits apart, breaks off and starts again as a new process unfolds. It is not an object but a flow. It is not linear but all pervasive.

"That flow seeks balance in all things until the puzzle of what is rests itself into the purest and simplest combination of what can be. It is an eternal jigsaw puzzle of arranging and simplifying the pieces until there are no gaps and no voids between them. When that happens, Love flows freely and evenly without pause.

"Move this piece here and that piece no longer fits over there. Turn that piece there to fit and another piece must be moved to make room for it.

"All of the pieces are in constant movement as is the board they are being played upon. They eternally change, coming together and breaking apart. You see this pattern in yourself and throughout your world.

"At some point, when all the energy has been burnished smooth and is pure of toxins, when there are no more moves to be made, every spirit fits together in harmony. That is the moment when there is nothing but the purity of Love left. That is the moment when all that is exceeds itself and a new cycle begins."

I could not help but think of birth and death, of the Big Bang and Genesis, and of the creation of our own universe regardless of whether viewed through science or religion.

At that moment I truly felt the ocean we sailed upon. My mind felt muddled with the waves. My thoughts rushed through my mind until they reverberated back from where they started as they reached the hardness of my skull toward the other side. It felt as if my own thoughts were interrupted by his.

"The human experience itself is forever evolving. It blossomed from the needs of a single point of consciousness. As more points of consciousness grew aware of the possibilities for discovery, the human experience expanded.

"That is the way of all things. Every cog is in constant motion. Each changes and evolves in its own way, yet in perfect synchronicity. Each was put in place and left to transform itself just as every species on earth transforms itself.

"The human experience is still at a very young point of in its consciousness. You are still of the earth. The earth is very much your home. Yet you have grown beyond your own boundaries. The crossroads you face are clear.

"One part of you yearns for the divine. The other retreats to the most primal of urges. You have a limited awareness for all that is, yet you understand there is more.

"Your ability to comprehend the entirety of the Universe is limited by the five senses you have grown to rely upon. It is as if you are a raindrop that has touched the ocean and you are in that moment just before you have entered it. Some see what is before them and smile. Others refuse to.

"You want to grow but you are still attached to the comfort of what you know. You want to attach rules and boundaries to what is beyond your comprehension. You want to understand the master plan for eternal existence, yet you fear to leave life.

"You want to see a finish line so that you can be comfortable as you continue to question and explore. You want to know that you are going in the right direction and that your life is not being wasted. Rest assured you are and it is not."

"You want larger answers but you are unsure how to ask the right questions. Be comfortable with your journey. You are here to experience existence with a limited perspective. You are here to learn the most simple of lessons about Love, compassion and understanding.

"It is not about the answers. It is about the questions. Some moments you will question ideas that you cannot even imagine. Each question is a step forward. Each question defines the answer, and each answer defines next question until you come to terms with the question you meant to ask in the first place. Only then can you realize the truth."

"Throughout it all remember, *'To thine own self be true'*. It is an idea that has resonated throughout the ages. There is another idea found in the ancient term *Ahimsa*. It means to do no harm. Each of these is a step in an evolution that connects the physical to something so much more.

"Each step is a bridge to the metaphysical as humanity rediscovers itself. With each step humanity takes, it continues to refine its experience so that each of us can find the purity that is within us. With each lesson humanity learns we remove that which is not Love so that we can collectively heal the void around us and re-weave the patchwork of existence.

"When you find your true self, you find your place in existence. It will be right where you started from, cleansed of all that is not you.

"Yours is a journey of ever-expanding consciousness and growing awareness. When all of existence aligns with of all the energies that are, there will be nothing left but Love. All else will be left behind. There will simply be."

Why is it that his words seemed to echo in every detail that I saw around me? Why is it that his thoughts seemed to shift my view, even if in an imperceptibly small way? Why did his simple words reverberate through my entire world?

I could not help but look over the side of the boat to see the individual waves lapping against the hull. I could not help but look out to see those individual waves flow into the pattern of the ocean and become lost.

As if catching my eye he interrupted my thoughts.

"Remember there is no difference between the movements of the ocean and the movements of the Universe. There is no difference between the Love of two people and the Love of all things. It is only a matter of scale. It is only a matter of perspective."

Those were the thoughts in my mind as I watched them gel within me. I watched them travel beyond my skull and into his being, I saw them fold with his thoughts before rebounding back to me. There was a transmission that I was unable to stop even if I wanted to. It was simply something I was aware of as I opened and we came together.

I could hear myself speaking before my lips ever moved. At first I thought to reach out and grab my thoughts before they escaped, but there was no time, nor was there any inclination. No matter how slowly they moved, they were out there and I could do nothing about it. Time was not an element here, there was something greater at play.

We both knew this. We also knew to mention this would be to destroy what was.

"Once you set an idea in motion it is not so easy to pull that energy back, is it? The energy of your thoughts exist long before you act on them. They exist whether you respond to them or not. They are just like everything else in existence. They are the pebble striking the water. They are the seeds for everything you are. They are what you are.

"Once you free your energy, even if it is but a thought, it is gone, out there in the Universe. Your intentions, your thoughts, are now a part of existence forever. You cannot take them back. You cannot undo them. You can only step into the flow and follow them. The key is to not think them in the first place. So that you do not have to spend more energy creating balance around them.

"Doing good does not erase doing bad. It may bring balance in the end. It may level the scales, but it will never stop the flow of energy. That is where the movements of existence come from. It is the eternal rebalancing of the energy that is that powers existence.

"Remember, energy can never be created or destroyed, it can only change form. That is why you must learn to be comfortable with the eternal imperfections of existence. The imperfections are what make the sea perfect. The constant movement that underlies everything is the stillness we all seek. There is no solid ground. There is only the comfort in the eternal currents and tides that exist in everything."

For a moment it was as if I had forgotten what his thoughts sounded like. It was not his voice, it was ours. Like the voice each of us has in the back of our heads only deeper. It was not heard so much as felt. It flowed through my body like wind or water. It didn't stop and start. It was a gentle current that connected me to the world around me, to the universe, to him, to myself.

"It is a gentle flow, isn't it?" I asked.

"It is. It mirrors everything in existence because it is existence. Physical, metaphysical, it all works together in perfect imperfection.

"When you are human the human experience is all there is for you. But it does not end there. It is not all that there is. You know this in your heart. It is your brain that seeks proof.

"All that you see, hear, taste, all of your world is a manifestation of the energy that your consciousness has created. It is the result of the waves that pass by and through your consciousness. Your world is the manifestation of the energy that is. It is created by the consciousness of the individual and held in place by the energy of the collective.

"It is up to you to choose your reality by the seemingly inconsequential decisions you make every minute of every day.

The energy is there for you to play with. How you perceive it is up to you. The emotions you perceive your reality through create your experience - for better or worse.

"When you are happy the sky is bright. When you are sad, the days are dark. The energy of the Universe gives you the day and the night. But it is you who make it as you see it.

"The collective consciousness of humanity gives shape and holds the world together as you see it. You refine it in the image of your own ever changing self. The Universe remains an open place with endless opportunities for growth and understanding. But it is you who makes it real.

"When you allow your ego to direct how you view your world, the energy around you becomes limited to the needs of that ego. The physical becomes all important. It closes to the energy of existence, to become limited to the desires of the moment and the fears for what may happen when that moment passes.

"Many follow their egos to see themselves as the center of their universe. They allow their perceived self-importance to blind them from the beauty and Love that is right in front of them. No matter what they acquire they realize it is nothing when compared with what could have been."

"There was a time when all of humanity thought of itself as the only thing in existence. As humanity grew the individuals within it realized there was more to existence than just them. For centuries they relegated themselves to just being at the center of the Universe. In doing so they limited themselves in their actions.

"As the human collective grew it saw beyond the artificial limitations that a few held so dear. Humanity soon realized there was so much more beyond borders and continents, even beyond the frail bubble that is earth.

"The more people realized what was out there; the more people realized the earth was not even a pinpoint in the celestial sky. At that moment a shift in understanding the true nature of the self occurred.

"The ancient Greeks conceived of the atom. For eons that idea was denied until the truth was proven. In time that idea was developed and expanded. Other discoveries grew from it. Smaller particles and forces for what is and what is not were conceptualized. That process continues to expand from the physical to the metaphysical, yet each holds true to the simple laws of existence."

"Understanding you are not alone and that you are endless is a step in your evolution. Understanding that you are part of the greater ebb and flow of existence is another. Acknowledging there is a collective consciousness that you belong to is yet another. Each of these is a lesson on the nature of existence.

"When you grow aware of the cycles of life that exist all around and within you, you become aware of the way in which the universe spins. When you see the universe as it is you begin to see what is beyond it.

"With that insight how can you think of the human life as the lone event of existence? It is not. It is simply one point in an endless line of evolutions.

"At one point your human body will cease to exist. That moment is far from the end of existence. That is far from the end of awareness.

"Well after your physical body ceases to exist, the energy that is you remains. The consciousness that gives form to your reality remains. Just as the end of a second does not stop time, the demise of the physical body does not stop life.

"Your consciousness continues, reflected in whatever form you take. When you are free from the limitations of the human experience, your energy will continue to expand on a deeper level than you could ever imagine."

"That is the beauty of existence. Existence moves in ways that you cannot even dream to comprehend. The form you are in at this moment allows you to witness the energy of existence through a very small window.

"It opens a door to the energy of existence in a limited way, so that you can begin to comprehend the limitlessness of all that is. The senses that you witness existence through are all you are capable of. As you grow, the paths that already exist will open to you; you will travel each at your own pace.

"Some people barely use the five senses given to them. Others open themselves to a sixth and a seventh sense. When you are ready more will appear. They transcend the human form. They leave growth eternally possible. It is there for you if you stay open to the reality of what is. Form and function are nothing without consciousness, awareness and spirit."

It freed me to hear him speak of the never ending cycles of life. It reassured me to see the waves from the boat, to remember the image of a hurricane seen spiraling from space. Even the image of our own Milky Way gave proof to his words about the circular nature of everything I knew. It was circles within circles.

"What about this dream? The boat? The here and now?"

"It is as real as anything else in your world. It is as real as you make it. If you allow an emotion to rule your life, that emotion will become your life. That emotion will become more real than the hardness of the earth around you.

"At times the very things you consider real are the most ephemeral. They will disappear to leave you with nothing more than a memory. For the remainder of your life that memory will be the most real part of your existence. Only later will you understand that it is like a breeze that moves unseen yet is profoundly felt.

"You see life in three dimensions. Four if you are aware of time. As you grow and evolve, you will see that there are many more to be explored. Each will open to you as you grow ready for them. Before that point, realize that the physical is not all there is. It is a reflection of the energy that is you."

"Before there was your physical self, the universe was existence without form. It remains a reflection of your consciousness. Everything, every person around you, is connected through a single point of consciousness, and all of this rests on the energy of Love.

"No matter what happens Love will always be there. It is energy without beginning or end. It is a part of the constant that ebbs and flows in eternal circles, just as the energy of Love ebbs and flows for all eternity.

"It is as if you reached over the boat and pushed the water aside with your hand. The ocean fills that empty space so quickly you can hardly see that there was once a point when nothing was there.

"The moment that vacuum is created energy flows in to fill it. Just as water moves to fill a hole left by a stone, the energy of Love fills the emptiness that is created. Perhaps a star is formed in that rush of energy. Perhaps an entire universe. Perhaps a new born life.

"On the level of existence the vacuum left by a lack of Love is filled at an unimaginable speed. It is filled before it is even empty. The force of its movement destroys what was but creates anew. The ocean remains the same, but it has also changed. How you perceive that change depends on your perspective."

I did not reach my hand over the side. I wasn't afraid to, but I was. I did not want to create a new universe with the dip of a finger. I simply wanted a moment to pause and rest.

"At that point do we actually die?

"Your question should be 'at what point do you start to live?'" He replied.

"There is no death. There is only growth, transformation. Suns are born and suns fade. At times the birth of a star is imperceptible. At others the splitting of an atom is cataclysmic. It all depends on the vantage point from which you view them.

"The key is that the balance of energy remains the same. That is where reality truly exists. It is found in the balance of energy that we are all a part of.

"To understand this you must expand your perspective to view existence from a greater distance. When you do you will see that linear thinking is limited thinking. That existence is a web without straight lines. There is no time, there is no death. There is only energy."

"Your idea of life is based on your perception. That is a window that only opens onto a very small garden. It is a sliver of all that existence is and can be.

"The concept you have of life is what gives substance to time. It is a linear idea that gives you comfort. There is a beginning and an end. With a perspective based solely on the human experience, and made real by the five senses that you have open before you, you begin to see everything in terms of minutes and seconds. You see the beginning and end of each day. You view life with a start and with an end. But existence goes on well beyond the point where your body has returned to the earth.

"The life of a body is but a moment in existence. The human experience is just one breath on the path of consciousness. Life as you see it is awareness from a single perspective. When your consciousness grows too great for your body, it expands beyond the limitations that are inherent in that body.

"You will find that your spirit, your energy, has many more cycles to explore on its journey. You will see that true life is as limitless as the energy that we all exist in."

Looking up and seeing the infinite stars in the black of the sky, I felt as if I were a part of that larger spiral of space and time. If I were to compare my life to the lives of the limitless stars out there, then he was beyond right. If I were to compare the life of a star to an eternity, it I would be staggering.

"When will that happen?"

He seemed to smile at me, "It happens all the time. It never stops. It will happen when you are ready for it to happen.

"The lessons you are here to learn do not form a list. They are experiences that fold into one another. They are dreams that you would not even recognize, torn from the cloth of humanity you are wearing.

"Your ancestors once saw the world as a flat plane of land and sea. That is all they were aware of because that is all they could see.

"When they sailed beyond the horizon and returned home they realized the earth was greater than the curvature allowed them to be a part of. They started to see the giant circle upon which they lived rather than the flat plane of their past. That changed their perspective of space, and of time.

"They looked beyond the ball that was once their home and learned of the solar system. They learned of the galaxy and of the universe and of many universes.

"Each time one person opened up to the possibility of more, another said 'Stop, what could be more important than our village, our land, our earth, our universe?'"

"When you are small you are afraid to see beyond yourself; you are even more afraid to see within yourself. As you grow, you begin to see yourself reflected in those around you. Toward the end of your human experience you begin to look within yourself. You see, you complete your journey right where you started, but with a new perspective. Even today as humanity explores the idea of endless universes some recoil at the glimpse of existence beyond space and time.

"Life, the human experience, the spiritual nature of being, they are just walls created to comfort the mind. They are separated by a fraction of a moment in the eternal clock of existence.

"Some people are born with a perspective limited to the most basic of physical needs. They focus on feeding the body, protecting what they think is theirs, fighting for more. They become caught up in the politics of physical existence.

"Others are aware of the energies that are all around them. They wade into the pools of energy that are found in a river, in a mountain and within a stone. They grow sensitive to the energy of others. They become attuned to senses that have always been there all along, waiting to be discovered. They become aware of what is out there that cannot be seen or smelled or touched."

"Everybody enters their own human experience from a different point of consciousness. Some see more than others. Some understand less. Some feel the energies that bond us all together. Others refuse to believe those energies even exist.

"Those are the lessons that each will learn as their consciousness expands. Neither is better or worse. Neither is more or less advanced. It is not a linear timeline that one advances upon. Each learns the lesson when each is ready. When one grows aware of a new perspective they grow beyond their old concept of reality. They become enlightened. They evolve."

"It is more important to realize that consciousness is not static than it is to define what consciousness is. Consciousness does not follow a fixed timeline. It flows like water. It overflows the banks that once held it back to find its balance.

"It does not start or end with the body. The human experience is just one stage of our never-ending journey, forever simplifying and expanding. It is a step toward our true existence and our true life. Our human experience is there for our spirit to explore our truth so that our consciousness will evolve to purity.

"The journey we are all on is like a wave. It never stops. It evolves from one existence to the next. It joins other waves. It leaves something behind as smaller waves for others to ride.

"Each of those smaller waves begins its own journey forever merging and breaking apart. Carrying part of our consciousness with it. Forever linked.

"Once we understand that we are all part of the same ocean, the boundaries disappear. When we encompass that with our mind, our spirit is free to ride a whole new level of awareness."

"It is not an easy concept to understand because the human equation wants to set boundaries for everything. Boundaries create a false sense of comfort. They remind you of your own skin, which is not there outside of the human experience.

"In truth there are no boundaries to the natural order of existence. There are only circuits and currents and connections. Where two planes meet there is turbulence, but always a flow.

"The shore is not a boundary for the ocean. Both land and sea exist in an eternal dance as storms create and erase the beaches.

"To humans those beaches are the boundaries, but life is not about separation. Neither is existence. Those beaches are found in the ebb and flow of all things, but the energy travels on. The human body is just the vessel that carries you on your path through existence."

I thought of his explanation and no longer saw a path in the woods, but an airy adventure through clouds, each opening and creating a path to the next space in time.

At that moment my journey stopped being linear. It became open to the endless visions and endless opportunities that are.

"Is this the path to enlightenment?"

"Path? No. This is the journey *of* enlightenment.

"There is no moment of enlightenment. Enlightenment is all around us. There are moments of enlightenment that occur well before your energy finds its place in the vastness of existence.

"Enlightenment is attained in every experience your spirit endures. Enlightenment is the humble opening of awareness. It is not relegated to the special or the holy. It is not a secret held for the deserved or for the learned. There are no rituals that must be performed. Enlightenment is the opening to the truth of existence. Enlightenment is the realization of awareness which you gain of yourself and your place in the oneness of existence.

"To be enlightened simply means to see beyond your own boundaries. It is to see your true self in existence. When you are able to do that you will see that every experience is open to you. It is there for you to reach out and explore.

"The act of understanding that you are one with everything around you is a moment of enlightenment. The act of understanding that the joy and Love that exists in the smallest of atoms and in the vastness of the Universe is another moment of enlightenment. Acknowledging your true existence free from hate and anger and darkness is yet another enlightenment. In the end, enlightenment does not matter. Where you take your enlightenment does."

"What happens to those who can't find enlightenment?"

"Enlightenment is inevitable. Enlightenment is not a state you work toward. It is a state that we all inevitably pass through. The question is not 'will you become enlightened?' The question is 'how arduous will your journey be through enlightenment?'

"Just as there is no evil to existence, there is no darkness to enlightenment. There is simply Love which you will find. It is inevitable. In the same way, the moments of enlightenment you pass through will lead to transcendence in the end."

"Just as there is no bad energy in existence, there are no bad people in the human experience. There are only frightened people who act badly because they have were taught to respond to life that way.

"These are people who have been trained through life to act out of fear. They mistakenly think it eases their pain when in reality it only adds to their pain and prolongs their journey.

"They are not bad in their hearts. They are only human. They have trapped themselves in a cycle of pain and fear that they have become comfortable in. They have learned that when they strike out and act badly they receive the attention they think they crave. That attention makes them feel good, but it lacks the Love they truly want.

"It is the same when a child throws a tantrum. When they do, they feel noticed. When they get what they want they quiet, they are trained that a tantrum is the path to what they think is Love.

"They do not realize that what they receive is not Love. When they do, they become more unhappy with each tantrum they throw. They receive, but they are not fulfilled with what they receive. They are happy for a moment but inside they are still empty.

"No matter what they have they have not been given the Love they seek. They have been given a replacement for Love. In time they become angry and resentful and empty. That is not their nature. It is how they have learned to act."

"Whether a criminal or a child, each is trained to act so that they feel noticed, as if they have left a mark. They feel they have created an event by which others will remember them. What they eventually realize is that it is the void that people recognize in them, not the energy. It is that void which holds them back.

"For some, that is a lesson of their journey."

We both seemed to pause.

"The angrier we are, the worse our existence becomes."

I spoke to myself, not realizing I spoke to him too.

He seemed to smile at my comment. Not for its humor, but for missing the larger direction we were moving toward. He looked around as if searching for something, an example perhaps.

I looked away for a moment, up to the night sky. When my gaze returned to the small cockpit of the boat, he was gone, and I was distinctly aware of the feeling of wood beneath me.

The rough, weathered grain was more apparent than it had been before. Perhaps my awareness was now more focused on the wood than it had been, but the sun-bleached blue and red of the paint was suddenly everything to me.

Beneath it his words and his thoughts echoed. I was left to contemplate all we had said. It was a lot. But I knew there would be more.

Once again I was made acutely aware of how perception makes things more or less real. Not because they were more or less real, but because we perceived them to be so. We acknowledged them to be of greater or lesser substance. And thus to each of us they were.

I waited for the next wave to lift the stern of the boat up. It slid beneath her hull as I pushed the tiller away from me. I consciously turned the boat back toward the wind and the harbor. I pulled the sail in, and she settled once again into the sea.

The scupper dipped toward the surface. A small spray of water arched out with each wave as we raced back toward the stone jetty that lay somewhere beyond the horizon.

I knew we would never make it before I found the sheets of my bed. We somehow never did.

FOURTH DAY

I knew when I woke that our trip had moved past its midpoint. It was not in anything that was said or done that I found this, but in the rise of energy that was palpable in the people of our house.

There was an undercurrent, not of desperation, but of a desire to see more, to do more. It was as if now that the impending departure times had become real, there was talk of things to see and to do.

There were pleasant nods and smiles as we each prepared our teas and coffees. There was talk of the world. There was also talk of sights to see and hikes to take.

Each of us disbanded into informal groups, and plans were laid out for the day. Less a series of plans really and more a general consensus of when we would all meet for lunch.

Some of us lingered around the house. Some went to beaches we had not yet visited. Others wanted to visit the ruins of the School of Homer and the Cave of the Nymphs. I was of the later group.

We all knew that inevitably we would meet back at the cafe at some point in the afternoon and then roam to wherever the winds would drive us.

On one hand, the ruins themselves were like any other of the countless ruins we had seen in our travels. Tremendous blocks of stone strewn about in massive squares that reflected the buildings and structures they once were. The remnants of columns pointed to what were once entry ways and were now rubble.

What always astounds me about structures dating back some three thousand years is that three thousand years ago someone had actually been able to craft and move and lift these massive blocks into different structures, and that some of that structure had actually survived through to the present day.

Amidst the ruins were the ever present goats. Only here they took on a whole new form. They were not the same animals we had seen before. They stood on branches and stretched their bodies upward to nibble on the leaves above. Their bodies almost appeared human, taking on ethereal shapes as they climbed onto the trunks of the old olive trees. We knew each of us were thinking the same thing, that this was where the idea of satyrs leapt into the minds of the ancient Greeks.

We took a path from the ruins of Homer up into the hills. We did not think about where we were going, we simply wanted a different vantage point before joining the others.

It was a hike that none of us were prepared for. Shorts and sneakers were no match for brambles and scraggly thorns in the heat of the day. We had all thought about turning back, but by the time one of us was willing to admit defeat, we spied an ancient grain tower that marked the summit of the island.

In the end we were glad we made the effort. Scratched and parched we stood on a landscape that was from another world. Stretched out before us, in all 360 degrees lay a sight like no other. There was endless blue water in a textured carpet that undulated with the waves that were. Rising out of it were islands of green and brown. It was similar to the view we saw on our ferry ride over, but now completely different.

We knew the landscapes of those islands. We had memories of our own that layered each with texture and life. They were no longer two-dimensional spots of color. Now they were real. We had seen the towns and sat at the cafes. We had spoken to the people. They were vibrant and rich with life. There was an energy to them that made them more than a smear of colors. They were alive with rocks and goats and people and olive trees.

We spent that afternoon on a rocky beach, collecting stones that caught our eyes, making up stories about the fissures and cracks worn smooth by the waves. We were touched by the sea that day. We simply could not help it.

FOURTH NIGHT

The Moments of Creation

On this night my dream had a feeling of sudden awareness. It was as if I woke up in the middle of a thought. I was not quite sure how I got there or how long I had been in that particular thought, but I was acutely aware that I was already well into my journey. It was as if I had daydreamed in the middle of our conversation and was now back aboard our little craft.

I was calm and relaxed in a way that only happens once you have sailed for hours. My back was burrowed well into my familiar corner of the cockpit. The boat was moving with the breeze. There was no heel and no wake, instead the hull gently moved with the motions of the waves; a part of the sea.

My eyes focused on the edge of the sail. It was more a habit than anything else. I was conscious of how it caught the wind without straining against the mast or the shrouds. It was full but not pulling as it was before.

I allowed my focus to drift up above the mast, to a higher place. The night sky and the sea beyond were calm and flat.

There was a breeze but no wind. There was a current, but no waves to speak of.

The boat rocked gently on its own pendulum. Its movements were like a breath, smooth and easy with a rhythm and a pace only the boat understood.

I looked around at the stars in the sky. They were reflected in the calm of the water as well. And yes, he was there as he had always been. It was as if neither of us had left the boat as somehow the world had settled in around us.

The more aware I grew of my surroundings the more I began to think that we were no longer on the water at all. Instead, we were floating somewhere between the sea and the sky. Above were stars. Below was the reflection of those stars or perhaps points of luminescence. They could have been the same except for the slight waver as the smallest ripples passed by unseen.

I took that moment to reach over and dip my hand into the darkness. It was cool and wet. Not icy as I knew the Atlantic to be, but not warm like the tropics. It was like touching a cool breeze, slightly chilly at first but then warming into something you never want to leave.

For that moment there was nothing to may entire existence except that point where my finger touched the water. I thought of the Buddha, and the statue where his fingers touched the earth while deep in meditation. I was so caught up in the sensation of touch that I hardly heard his voice as they entered my thoughts.

His voice was less a sound than a sensation. It was like the water, as if felt through a different medium; one that transcended the senses without limiting the breath.

"The laws of the Universe are the same whether you know of them or not." was all he said.

"Then why not just teach them as they are?" I asked?

"It is not enough to recite the laws of physics or of faith. To truly learn you must experience each. To cross from the physical to the metaphysical every moment of your consciousness must experience what it is to be finite and infinite.

"It is the moment that a raindrop touches the surface of the ocean. It can either let go of the walls that maintain its form and hold on to sense of being a drop, or it can let go of its former self and enter the ocean it hovers above.

"You are no different. You can ride upon the surface of the ocean without ever entering, or you can let go and become a part of all that is. Without experiencing what it is to be infinite you would simply vanish into the depths of the ocean without enhancing it.

"Every experience provides you with a new perspective. Each expands your awareness to see that a single thought has many points of view. Each point of view is woven into the fabric of your existence and into the tapestry that is you.

"Your true self chose the human form in order to observe existence from a different vantage point. Each step in your journey brings you closer to your own divinity. You are not here to learn about the universe. You are here to learn about yourself. For your own divinity is the divinity in all that is."

"In the turbulence of formation, the purity of your spirit grew clouded. When you mature from being a child, you gain experience. The cost of that experience is innocence. You explore the wrong path. You make what you think are mistakes. Your mistakes haunt you until you realize there is no wrong path. Each misstep is a way for your true self to rediscover the right path that you should be on.

"It is all a part of your journey. The lessons you experience echo on through every level of your consciousness. As your consciousness grows you flow into new forms. As you grow turbulence is created. Voids form in that turbulence. The energy that flows through you stops or finds a new path. Every experience provides a new vantage point with which to reach across the void so that the Love of existence can flow again.

"The process of questioning and experiencing, of exploring, leads you back to clarity and purity. The human experience is but one perspective that brings you back to a point of grounding so that you may refine yourself and grow again."

I no longer needed to be led into the conversation. On this night I felt as if I was already immersed in the ebb and flow of our collective thoughts. I could feel his knowledge and experience run through me. I smiled and nodded as the thoughts stopped being mine or his. They became ours in a transference of consciousness.

"How did it all begin? What was the moment like when that first wheel began to turn?"

"How that first wheel began to turn is beyond our comprehension. Who knows how long the creator energy of

Love flowed until it reached the point that sparked consciousness into being. When that point of consciousness became aware, existence was born.

"In that moment that lasted an eternity existence was created, universes were formed. As consciousness expanded, the energy of Love overflowed its banks.

"Each universe continues to feed the expanding consciousness that is. Within each universe, elements join together and split apart. New and more complex elements are created. Galaxies sprout from the dust of stars as they tear apart and collide together. The building blocks reform and rejoin until life comes into being and then return to the nothingness that is eventually left.

"In the end the only thing that is left is the purity of consciousness. Between those points each universe is a classroom within which the consciousness expands.

"As a single point of consciousness expands so does the Love it rests upon. Its own awareness weaves the tapestry of existence. Each thread creates the cloth of being. It is a web of consciousness that ebbs and flows until it fits together without gaps and voids. It becomes tightly woven into the sea of Love."

And there it was I thought. There it is.

"With that first fraction of a thought existence is split apart and woven together again and again. In the briefest moment of time and space the elements that you accept as matter come into and go out of being. The threads of consciousness weave existence as the energy of Love flows freely through it.

"That moment of creation occurs at every level of existence. In that moment of conception there is purity. Voids form and it is only through Love that each is made whole again.

"Existence is simply the process of evolution. As a human you first lean to survive in the natural environment of earth. You learn to eat and breathe. You then learn to interact with those around you. You learn the order of the society you were born into. When you have experienced all there is to experience in the world you learn, once again, to survive in the environment of yourself.

"You will struggle with the layers you acquire as you learn your own Simple Truth. In that moment when you realize that your own Simple Truth is the truth of all existence, that is the moment you return to your beginning with a new perspective.

"This is a journey that we all repeat many times and on many levels. It is a journey that continues throughout the Universe and throughout existence. This is why the Universe was born from its creator's energy. From your energy. It was created for you."

"The pure energy that is you is still there. It always has been. This is the process of purifying and simplifying. It is the never ending process of cleansing and connecting. It is how you grow and evolve as a human to become the spiritual being you have always been.

"With every life we live and every form we take we mend another void. Those are the gaps that hold us back from joining the divinity that we all are. It is also what holds us from being part of the energy of pure Love.

"Some think of that moment as entering Nirvana or walking into the gates of Heaven. Some call it Jannah. Those are just different words for the same idea that is far too large to grasp.

"That place already exists all around you. It is not opened to you after someone judges you. It is recognized by you as you transcend on your path every day through moments of enlightenment that you enjoy."

Our thoughts echoed and reverberated. The very boundaries that formed the drop of my consciousness seemed to waver and dissolve as I became a part of the sea I had only just touched.

Before a drop can join the greater sea of existence that most basic drop must reach beyond its boundaries until it is no longer held back by its own sense of self. The very walls that helped it find its true truth now prevent it from being what it was meant to be all along.

It is not one or the other that is the goal. It is the duality of both. It is retaining its individuality while remaining open to the enormity of all. In the end we are all drops seeking to join the ocean without losing the Love that makes us what we are.

"Oh, to remove the boundaries that make me human," I thought.

"To remove a boundary you must first recognize the boundary. With every boundary you find, you also find a path to the divinity within. Simply being aware starts the wheels of purity in motion. Each experience moves us closer to the simplicity we seek in the end.

"Every step of our existence is a lesson that brings us one step closer to the Love that is already in us. It flows through us. It connects us. We simply have to stay open to it."

I became aware of those moments when I was open to the adventures of the world. I remembered what it felt like when I shut down and drew into myself. I felt how small it made me feel, or how it made me not feel at all.

"When we were a rock we had little awareness of the world around us. It was so for a reason. That moment of eternity enabled our true self to focus on just one aspect of our energy. We witnessed the pressure of the earth as it pressed upon us. We spent a millennia moving from mountain, to river, to sea. We felt the effects of surf and tide reduce us to an individual grain of sand. We felt each grain join together to become a beach. We learned that individual grains can form a greater end.

"We grew and evolved as we polished and buffed the layers that held us back. We continue to eternally evolve and simplify as new forms await. With each new form and each new experience, new lessons are learned until the energy that is transcends into the point of consciousness we came from.

"It is through our existence that we return to being a rock or see life through the eyes of a child once again. Each helps us to refine our energy. With every level of existence we become aware of our continued growth. We become aware of the evolution that waits for us. This does not happen in the future, but in the here and now.

"Every cycle of existence enables us to experience our energy in a new way. With each we resolve and mend the questions of being. We gain awareness of the new experiences that are there.

"For some the experience of a life lasts just 24 hours. That is enough. For others viewing a cocoon through the eyes of a child is an experience that lasts an eternity. Each lesson is a lesson learned from a new and different perspective.

"That is the beauty to it all. There is no schedule to meet. There is no winning. There is no losing. There are no goals; there is no one waiting to judge before we enter the sea, because we are already a part of it.

"There is simply the never-ending wheel of consciousness that expands with each experience we pursue until it leaves us to rejoin the sea of Love that is all around. That we are already a part of"

And so it went for me. I became comfortable with our shared thoughts. Less a conversation and more a meeting of the minds. The moment I thought I understood was the moment I realized there was more. And I wanted more. It was that knowledge that helped me understand that I was back at the beginning of a new conversation; one that never ended.

"We see, yet in so many ways we do not see. We give up the idea of solid land. We give up the idea of a single line. We are free to follow the currents of energy wherever they lead. We are free to flow in an endless sea of experiences.

"When we are comfortable reaching out in every direction we learn there are new planes to explore. We weave a tapestry with threads of Love, knotted in points of consciousness.

"We are all a part of an ever-changing, ever-evolving experience. One that exists in a cycle within a cycle that runs parallel to yet another cycle. They touch. They cross. But they never meet. It is we who are the connecting points between those cycles.

"This is how existence works. We are all interconnected in a series of links where the physical and the metaphysical worlds are the same. There is no difference between thought and being. Each overlap and flow into the next. As our consciousness connects them."

"Every morning you open your eyes your dreams do not end. They settle into our being as another current through which our collective consciousness expands. It is yet another path through the human experience.

"When your eyes open you once again become aware of your body and the world around you. You become aware of your five senses and the limits that come with them. But in your awakening you do not lose the dreams.

"Every night you return to sleep you leave the boundaries of your earthly body behind. Your mind is freed from the constraints of the physical world in which you live but not in which you exist.

"In your sleep you are free to explore without weight or touch or pain if you wish. You are free to blend and to morph as you want. The back and forth is a cycle we repeat every day. It is a window into the conscious plane that we all inhabit.

"When you are deep in sleep you do not cease to exist. Your body is there. But your consciousness is here. Your awareness opens a path between the two. You are given the freedom to be fully aware if you so choose. At that point you can recreate your world free from the constraints of your physical self, open to the possibilities that are.

"If nothing else, it is a reminder that you are both a physical being and a metaphysical energy. You have a physical body that has needs that you must attend to if you are to survive on the human plane of existence, if you are to pursue the hopes and dreams you set out to follow.

"There are lessons to learn and a destiny to reach. You cannot live without the one. We cannot grow without the other. Our existence is a duality dependent upon satisfying both the physical brain and the metaphysical mind.

"It is no wonder that you grow torn between the two. If you pay too much attention to the physical the spirit withers. If you pay too much attention to the spirit, the body is neglected. It is the balance between the two that you are here to learn. That balance is a lesson of enlightenment.

"Once you have found this for yourself, you are then to help others see. Discovering this duality while keeping a balance between the two is another step toward transcendence. It is a lesson to grow through as we all expand into the greater good without leaving the self behind."

I smiled at the thought and at the calm progress we were making to a destination that did not exist, but at the same time did. It was not a distant shore we were heading to, but an idea, a dream within a dream. And it was forming around us.

"That is why we are here." It came from within me.

"We are here for the same reason we are anywhere. We exist to explore and to discover. We exist to grow aware of the Love that we are each capable of. It is our awareness of that Love with which we reach out to those around us. It is those threads of Love that we connect with other, to knit existence together. In the end all that is, is the Love that is you. You return to the beginning in a simpler, purer form; more whole than when you began.

"Between the beginning and the end, between the alpha and the omega, between the first and the last each of us experiences what it is to be. We may become a rock or a flower or a bird or a fish. We may become beings we are not even aware exist, both of your world and not of your world. We take forms that provide us with the lessons we need to grow and evolve.

"Each experience helps us shed that which is not pure. As we grow we become aware of what is out there, we grow more aware of what is within. Like a skin that no longer fits we shed our old self as we pursue Love through the planes of existence.

"Freed from fear we are able to Love openly and freely. As our Love grows so do we. As we learn to replace the emptiness that fuels hate, envy and jealousy with Love, the layers that once slowed our journey fall away and our journey advances.

"Peel back the fear that blocks our collective energy from flowing and we peel back the very thing that keeps us bound to the human experience. As we expand, the emptiness is filled with Love. We become buoyant and rise like a balloon."

That image, the idea of a physical balloon brought me back to the boat we sat in. I smiled as I watched the wind carry us onward and seemingly upward across the water.

The hull of the boat no longer cut through the water but was a part of it. The black of the hull mirrored and became one with the sea we traveled upon.

"Always remember, the Universe is a very simple place. Eternity is as well, if you allow it to be. The rules of nature apply equally to everyone and everything. Just as physical bodies rise when they are freed from the weight that anchors them. The spirit does the same. That is our journey, to lighten our spirits so that we can soar.

"When we are happy we feel light and invincible. It is the same when we are in Love. We are no longer weighted down with the imbalances of life. We are no longer blocked by the voids of existence.

"Our respective journeys are never about shedding negative energy. It is about balancing the Love within us to the Love that is without.

"With each connection within and without we create currents that fill the emptiness. We become a spirit of Love that is in balance with the Love of existence."

"The beautiful part of this wonderful experience is that we do not have to wait to find the Love we all seek. It is here all around us. The actions we take today create the energy we live in tomorrow.

"It is not that bad actions which creates bad energy. Those actions create no energy at all. They simply create voids that stop the flow of energy. Those voids result in new cycles that we must then expend our own energy to overcome. It is why a bad action ends in turmoil for us, turmoil that we must calm before we can move on.

"Good actions results in the positive flow of Love through which our journey can continue. We create bridges over which our energy flows right here and now. We can enjoy our blessings the moments we create them. We do not have to wait for the some final moment of positive energy. That moment simply flows with us with every thought we make. At any time we can escape our boundaries and experience the Love that is. Whenever we want."

There was a momentary shimmer to the deck of the boat. It may have been a star reflecting on the wet and shiny wood. It may have been a trick of my eye seeing a ripple in a star reflected in the calm water.

From one star I saw another and another as my awareness grew. It was like watching the stars and the sea unfurl all the way to the horizon. Not as reflections of each other but as one.

My attention glimpsed my hand on the tiller. I gently pushed it away from me as if it was not my own. The boat turned as I did. I pulled it back and regained our course. Even though our course was set, my sense of self could still move us. In that moment I could hear my thoughts again as separate from ours.

"How do I share this?"

I could hear the voice of his thoughts join my own. Separate and distinct, but still one with mine.

"When you respond to a gesture positively you grow in the human experience. When you allow a piece of art to move you or when you find someone that inspires Love within you, your consciousness expands as does ours. You remain open as you discover the Love that is within you and within all things.

"When you look down upon someone as unworthy of your Love you close off a channel that was open for you. In that moment you find a small gap within yourself. The regret you feel is the loss of energy you witness. That block is caused by the small void you created.

"When you recoil from someone not as pretty as you think they should be, when you mock someone to make yourself feel better, when you keep someone below you to raise your self-esteem, the void within you expands. The anger you feel rise up is not anger for them, but for yourself. It is the recognition of the void you have seen within yourself."

"When someone you Love rejects you, it is not them you dislike. It is the void they have revealed within you. Your old brain becomes aware of the emptiness. It responds in the only way it knows how, with the emotions it has at its command.

"It is why you harden yourself against the pain and the loneliness you are sure will come. You allow that void to close yourself off from the circuit of Love that is all around you.

"What your very human brain does not realize is that pain is a part of life. It is not a part of existence. It will always be there in the human experience.

"That is okay. It means you are alive. It also means you have more lessons to learn, to let it go of, and to replace with Love. If you allow the void within you to fill with anger that void will only grow.

"If instead you fill the void with the joy and Love that is in your life, your pain will ease; the void will mend. That is the only way for a tragedy to become a positive force in your life. One which you will grow and evolve from.

"The events in your life reveal the emptiness that is within you. How you respond to those events is what fills the emptiness or allows your Love to expand.

"The way you respond to the world around you is a reflection of the Love within you. When you become aware of your actions, you learn to transform them into positive energy. When you do that your consciousness grows.

"As your consciousness grows, so does your awareness. When your awareness expands beyond your boundaries, you are freed to reach deeper and to surpass your boundaries. That is the moment your participation in the Love that is becomes greater.

"It is like a snowball that rolls down a hill. It builds and grows. If you stay open to the flow of Love, you will open yourself up to experience the Love of existence."

I blinked into my own awareness. With everything that had gone on in my life, his words seemed to be a summary of my responses. It was like the wavelets upon the waves upon the currents of the sea. There was a pattern to them as they broke away and sailed off on their own. The pattern was simple on the surface, yet deeply layered just beneath.

I thought about Love and existence, about simple responses amplifying the depths into the easy flow of the surface. His being smiled into a nod. His thoughts followed the path mine created.

"The Love that lies between two points of consciousness is the same as the Love that connects two people," he intoned.

"Everything we experience is a reflection of the Love we create in the universe and across existence. The Love felt between two people is the Love that connects their two points of consciousness. Every time we open up and accept Love, we experience the current that is created. That current connects the edges of a void to create a new path upon which to explore.

"To explore that path we must simply stay open to the possibilities of all that could be. We must trust. We must respect. We must accommodate. We must Love.

211

"Love grows within us because we allow it to. Even if we do not acknowledge it we have faith in the Love that is. When we come upon a void, the emptiness before us creates the fear and self-doubt. That is the moment we pull back and allow our Love to fade.

"Many times we lack the strength to stay open to the Love within. We give into the void because the fear of being hurt is too great. That fear causes us to close down and retreat into the safety we think lies within our physical self. We create our own prison within the human experience.

"It is in that prison that we experience pain from the loss. But no matter how great the pain we retain the memory of what it feels like to Love, because cannot separate ourselves from the Love that is undeniably our nature.

"As we extend Love across the void we see before us, we reach out to connect with others. Each smile, each touch is a way to connect.

"When the Love we put out returned we find that we are able to step past our fears. We find that the void we once dreaded is not quite as vast as we once thought. We find that staying open to Love is easier because of the Love being returned from the other side. In that moment we mend the sea of existence by weaving those small threads into a tapestry that will hold any weight. We grow with the incredible energy of what can be.

"That moment is why we are here. That moment is what happens across the planes of existence whenever two energies come together. Whether it is two galaxies uniting, two streams joining into a river, or two cells becoming one, it is the same.

"It is Love."

"The metaphysical and the physical are the same, are they not?" I asked?

"Just as your physical actions reflect the thoughts behind them, your thoughts reflect the energy behind them. When it is real and true, the physical act of making Love reflects the bonds that are woven across the sea of existence.

"The spiritual union enjoyed by two people when they are truly in Love transcends the five senses and opens us up to see all of existence. To some it is a spiritual awakening. To others it is a conduit through which a new level of awareness flows.

"It is why so many cultures see the act of making Love as a spiritual practice. They recognize the eternal joining of energies that are reflected within that act of making Love. They witness the Love that is channeled and smile.

"Some recognize the divine female as a reflection of the energy that created it all. She is the channel through which two divine selves can join, through which a new cycle of energy is spun into existence. They see the moment of conception as a divine moment that is no less miraculous than the creation of a star. Every step that a child takes toward maturity is a divine moment that should be celebrated in its own right.

"It is the same as when a spirit moves on from the human form. It is the same as when a spirit grows and expands. Each step fulfills a divine destiny, each a divine moment of celebration."

The boat creaked and groaned as the breeze stiffened ever so lightly. There was not enough force to keep everything tight. Instead, the wood ached against its joinery. It reminded me that even boats were living things, complete with the energy of the wood and the Love that made them.

The realization of the physicality seemed to separate us once again into the back and forth of a conversation rather than the oneness of a single thought.

"What happens when two people stop loving each other?"

"Two beings never truly stop loving each other. The Love is always there. It will always be there. It may not look the same, but it is there for them if they are willing to overcome the fear they have of reaching out and being rejected. If they want to see the Love that is they simply have to overcome the fear within and accept the Love without.

"The hate, the anger, the fear you think is there does not really exist. It is simply the very human realization of what the lack of Love will bring. The hate and anger you feel is your body trying to comprehend the total void of Love before them.

"Instead of sending a string of Love and hope across the void, it is as if each stands looking down into the abyss before them rather than up to create a connection across the abyss.

" It is the fear of emptiness that you pull away from, not the person across from you. Inevitably, and in time, a bridge will inevitably be woven into a bridge. When that is done, you can reach across and rejoin.

"When a pebble is dropped into a pond there is a momentary void created. That emptiness is quickly filled from all sides as water rushes in. The sea of existence acts no differently. It mirrors this on an infinitely larger scale. The emptiness is filled in as the Love of existence rushes to create balance.

"Every time Love disappears from our lives an opportunity opens before us. We have a chance to witness emptiness. We also have a chance to heal that emptiness. We can weave a new connection, or we can hide in the void that is."

"We are healed with every step we take into the sea of Love. With each step our very human brain echoes its fear against the potential for pain and loss. We remember all the pain we have ever felt from the past bubble up in an effort to avoid it instead of the joy.

"In time we begin to remember the joy. We weigh the two until a balance is reached. In time we find another spirit that tips the scale of Love over pain. Our very human self deems that as a person who is worth the risk. In the end we leap in with little more than faith and hope and Love. That is when we truly smile.

"You see, the same rules apply no matter how big or small the hurdles appear to be. The water fills the void of a pebble. It does not think about how much space there is to fill. It simply flows until the void is filled, and then it overflows to cover the void completely.

"When you first meet someone you do not ask how much Love they need. You simply give until they are filled. Then, if it is true Love, you give more. You fill the void until it overflows, and like water, your Love takes the form of whatever is before it.

"You ask yourself again and again, "Is this true Love?" "Is this what Love truly feels like?" There is not a single sight or a sound or a taste that tells you this is true Love. It is an all-encompassing energy.

"Even without your senses, you recognize Love. It is palpable. It is real. You can sense it in two people. You know when they are in Love and when they are not.

"Animals can sense when there is a kinship. Beasts show affection even to species that are not their own. Humans are no different. Love is not physical. It is not confined to a single sense. Is all encompassing. It is all around. It simply is."

I am not sure how long we sat there absorbing his words that now seemed to echo my thoughts. We watched the steady movement of the boat and felt the light breeze as it moved us forward. Minutes or hours may have passed. It was hard to tell when there is nothing to tell time by.

There was something in what he said that made me pause. I think it made mankind pause ever since we started. My dreams now surpassed my basic need for sleep. Even within my dreams I realized that this was more. Perhaps it was the spirit of Homer that fed the question to me.

"If we are returned to Love no matter what happens in our human experience, does that mean we have no Free Will?"

"That there is a destiny for you does not mean your life is pre-written. It is inevitable that you will end up where you started from. What path you take is entirely up to you. And that is what will make all the difference. That is what will create the human experience for you.

"You can change your life and experience at any time with the smallest thought or action. Having a destiny simply means that in the end the human experience you pass through will bring you one step closer to uncovering your true self.

"There are endless paths upon which to journey. Each leads to the same destination. Each will unpeel a layer that prevented you from actualizing your true self. It is why it is the journey that is all important, not the destination."

"As each of us travels on our journey, we discover that the closer we travel to Love the less limited that Love becomes. When we first discover Love in the human experience, we do not think of everyone. We think of ourselves and what Love is doing to us. Each of us looks at Love as if it is only we who are able to experience it in this way.

"As we grow we begin to understand that Love is not a fixed ideal. It comes in many forms and at many levels. We understand our own need to find Love. We also understand the desire to become a part of a larger consciousness if we are to experience it on a deeper level.

"When we do, that is a point when the individual ends and eternity begins. It is the difference between finding God and knowing God.

"It is the start of a new cycle. One that begins exactly where the hold one began, but with greater experience. We began as individuals. We end as a collective. This collective becomes the new individual, only larger. It has just as many facets, just as many points of confusion. All of which will inevitably be polished down as we travel on our journey together.

"In the end my experience is the same as your very human experience. Look within yourself. Even in your own reality you are not an individual. You are a collective of cells and bacterium that all work together to keep your very human self alive.

"Have you ever wondered why there are so many facets to your personality? Have you ever wondered why there is such inner conflict? You were once so many different individual points of energy now trying to work as one. In the human experience there are many elements that work to unite each of those parts. Age is one way. Decay is another.

"Being aware of your body and mind as you mature is to be aware of the inevitability of your physicality. You learn what it is for the flesh to die and for the spirit to awaken. The physical and the divine begin to mirror each other. As you uncover one, you discover the other. Together each reveals the simple truth that is your true nature.

"This is your destiny. It is for you to write your journey. For some it may take days or minutes. For others am entire lifetime, for others still, it may take many. The number of cycles each of us needs is not important. Time is not a part of this journey.

"Having an inevitable destiny simply means that there is no failure. There is simply a place to which you will eventually arrive. That is the inevitability of existence. In the end all of existence will be in balance, ant that balance will spark a new beginning.

"When you reach your destiny the whole beautiful cycle will begin again on an entirely new level. You are a wavelet. You will experience wind and tides. You will give birth to a new wavelet as you peel off from the wave you were riding. You will endlessly explore as each part of you is reborn. It is a beautiful cycle that never ceases. This is the essence of being."

Looking up at the billions of stars that filled the skies, I smiled at the image he created. It was as if every star in the sky was a tiny light powered by the electricity of Love.

At that moment I felt as if every turbine in the world was powered by Love. As if the fuel that sparked our cars was not based on the decomposed bodies of ancient creatures but by the Love that at one point in time was found within them.

I understood that we truly were all made from stardust. That our entire world was powered not by the physical but by the seemingly obscure source we always knew about but rarely acknowledged. It was no different from the winds or the sun that energized our planet.

It was a moment of awakening. It came not as a thunderclap or a lightning bolt, but as a steady flow of energy that rustled the leaves of my spirit. It was a gift that has always been there. But here I was, feeling as if I just tapped into it for the first time.

The proof of his words was found in every cell of my body. It was found in the suns that powered the planets; that heated the air, and caused the ocean currents to flow. It flowed from a light switch to a bulb and powered life on a scale I could not imagine. It was connected and linked because it was all the same. It all simply depended upon the vantage point from which you witnessed the great world spin.

I lay back and felt the wood of our small craft press into my back. I let my mind go and watched as it expanded further than I had ever allowed my mind to go before. I realized that on such a scale something far more universal was needed than the power of electricity, or solar, or mechanical, or even nuclear if it was all to be brought together. The universe required something far more universal, and the plane of all existence?

Well, when I settled into that realization another one rose. I smiled at it as it took form and became real. I looked up to find my partner was no longer sitting there. I hardly expected him to be. He no longer needed to be. He was all around.

I didn't worry that I had no wind to power my sails. I realized that on this sea it was never the wind that powered them in the first place. I gently lay my head back on the railing of the boat. I watched the top of the mast gently sway back and forth to the small arcs of the waves. It created a pattern all its own against the stars above.

I fell asleep in my dream to that gentle sway. The mast moved slowly against the dark bluish black of the sky and the ever twinkling stars fueled on the batteries of Love.

FIFTH DAY

It was from my within my dream's dream that I woke to my day. When I eventually opened my eyes, I did so with a smile as I settled into the sun and the breeze. The sound of French drifted in from the yard. It was mixed with the sounds of the goats and the energy of the island itself.

Our friend and hostess was singing in a sweet voice, so well defined and distinct. I could not understand all of the words, just enough to know they were about the events of the day ahead. I lay there, content with not understanding everything, but able to discern something beneath the words. It was as if another conversation was going on beneath the punctuation.

I lay there in that wonderful place between dream and physicality. I was on the bed, yes, but when I closed my eyes I was on the boat again. My body rested on the gentle rise and fall of the water as I watching the energy of the world drift by.

I was here. That much I knew. But I was un-tethered. I could feel the limits of my body on the raw linen of the sheets. I could feel part of me transcend those sensations. It was as if an umbilical cord still connected me to that dream, refusing to let me fully return to the world.

My breath filled my lungs. My heart continued to beat. But the rest of me was gone. It was as if I didn't exist except as a thin vessel that lay between the air in the room and the air within me. The deeper I breathed, the thinner I became. I was still physical, but I was no longer a barrier between the two worlds.

What there was of me floated on the emotions that drifted in the air until even those left to become a part of the murmur that was all around.

It was a beautiful feeling to behold. Being, but not being. Solid, but ethereal. Alone, but connected. I was floating between. I was here yet not really.

I was aware of the sea of energy that was all around me. I was also aware of my own energy. I was connected but still an individual.

I'm not sure how long I lay there. I am not sure if I stayed awake or drifted back to sleep. Time was not really a part of me.

When I finally woke to the physical world, I wrapped myself in a sarong and joined the day. It was sunny and bright, but a different kind of day. I knew it was not the day that was different. It was me, and I smiled into that.

The ground rose up to meet my feet. The sounds that drifted on the breeze were of the day and the insects. Even the scents and the light gave me the earth what was all around. It was as if my senses were no longer confined to their distinct boxes of smell and sight, touch and hearing as they always had been.

Each flowed back and forth. Scents augmented my vision. Vision heightened my touch. Touch increased my awareness of the vibrations that were all around me.

Even my morning ritual of making tea and toast became something more. It was as if the tea itself had opened up to reveal itself to me. The taste, the heat, the water, all washed in the hues of the tea were distinct as each flowed into my cup.

Each came alive in a way that I had always known but never seen before. Each was so distinct as to be a separate experience. It was singular as much as a collection of distinct subtleties.

I felt the quiet within myself that morning. Whatever I had to say was returned back to me. I did not speak; I watched as the world came to life. I watched myself come to life. When questions drifted about how I had slept, I simply told the truth. I told them that I had slept wonderfully and that I had had the most wonderful conversation on a boat in my dreams.

Tired of our separate adventures, we decided to spend the better part of our last day roaming the coastline of the island. We pulled into different coves and dropped anchor. We swam to the beaches and napped in the sand. We did not care if we were wet or dry, or if the sand stuck to us or not. We knew that the water would wash it all away when we swam, each stroke bringing us into a new experience.

Between strokes I dove down beneath the waves and took in the silence of the water. I could see particles suspended in the water as the light filtered down between them. It was as if the light itself was caught in the water, creating a bluish, green curtain of slow undulating waves. I could feel the energy around me, pass through me, fill me.

I observed that day as it gently passed into night. I listened to the patter of conversation during dinner. All of it from a distance, not really hearing the words but feeling the cadence, the pace and the tones.

I smiled at being a part of the conversation without speaking a word, simply enjoying the energy that passed back and forth, from one to another. It was the energy more than the words that kept the evening flowing and alive. It was the current of Love that I watched being shared as my wife laughed and smiled and enjoyed the pool of energy we all bathed in. It was Love through which we enjoyed our food and each other's company.

It was with that energy that I went to bed. As I left them on the deck, I saw their energy reflected in the candlelight and in the starlight and in the conversation as it drifted from French to English. The Love we all shared was a part of the simple connection of smiles and gazes and pleasantries.

I crawled beneath the sheets that night, sated as I tucked myself in. Knowing that night I slept under a canopy of Love.

FIFTH NIGHT

Transcendence

When I woke from my dream of daytime there was no ocean surrounding us. There was no sky above. There was simply a flow of energy that ran around us and through us. It was as if I was floating at the center of existence. No, not floating, being.

Even though there was nothing around me, I felt the ebb and flow of the tides, the winds and the motion of the waves. The stars, once reflected in the water, were the water. The waves that rocked the boat were the boat. It was only then that I truly realized that the boat I had grown comfortable with was no more. It was there, but not there. It was as if the boundaries that once existed were an illusion. The deck was there but without the wood of the deck or the paint of the seats.

The last vestige of my physicality left me as I realized that even the water lacked the wateriness of water. It felt like the purple blackness of the night sky. The stars floated in the sky like particles suspended in the sea. The sea itself blended with the sky, and the water, the air, and the boat. They were still distinct, but one.

My only thought was that we were drops that had just merged with the ocean of existence; that this is what it must feel like to be a part of existence but still separate. Independent but one with all in that moment before the last boundary releases.

I let go of my ego and realized this is what they mean when they talk about knowing God. My mind accepted the truth behind this conversation. It was a dream after all. But a dream in the real world that is.

At first I searched for something real to hold on to, before I realized I was just grasping. Everything around me was real, more real than anything I had ever known before.

I grew comfortable with the thought that it was not the boat that I needed, but the idea of the boat. I realized that I did not need the wooden railing or the hull. I did not need the sails or the keel. I only needed my own center to find the balance I so needed.

I let go of my fears and allowed myself to sink into what was. It was not water or boat beneath me. The limits of our craft were gone. They were replaced by the comfort that came from within.

I knew I was safe. I was cradled in the hands of a mothering cocoon. The boundaries I once found comfort in were no more, but their energy remained stronger than ever.

There was the context of a boat, but there was no hull. I felt the rail against my back and the seat beneath my body, but there was nothing there. There was not even a depression where the water should have been.

It shocked me at first. Not the shock we feel when we panic. It was more like the shock you get when you taste the most incredible taste ever. It awakened me with a sense of incomprehension that left me wanting more.

I smiled as I realized that there was no more. There was no me to want more. There was no him for me to want more for or from. There was just we, and even that was limiting compared to what was offered.

There was an energy where my friend once sat as he always had. There was no border between us and the sea. It was as if he and I were two points of water joined within the water itself.

At that moment I knew we were cradled, not in hands, but in Love. It flowed around me. It flowed through me. It was as if a flow of comfort and joy was all there was. Not in some dream state, but in a reality that was more real than I had ever known.

It was as if all there is was held in a subtle fold in the energy of existence. As if our awareness was but a ripple in the sea.

I was aware of a uniqueness to each of us, as if we were two drops in an ocean. Our differences were gone. Our uniqueness more prominent than ever in a way that showed a true collective, and it felt good.

"This is what is," we both seemed to say.

It wasn't a voice. It wasn't an emotion. It came from within, from my thoughts but also from outside of them. I knew it was our connection. My energy smiled, knowing, understanding, accepting, being.

It all comes from within. Everything experienced and explored echoes from within. Part is the reality of consciousness. Part is the consciousness we share. The less you create, the more open you remain to the energies that float past and through.

I gave in to it and allowed my consciousness to rest on his energy. I was aware there was no he or I or here or there. There simply was. Each was less a sense of self, as a sense of origin. There was a sense of belonging with nothing separating us. There was everything whether it was from within or without.

It was like watching thoughts form in a meditation free from beginning or end, simply an endless flow to touch upon. There was a feeling of Love and ease and comfort and awareness. There was an incredible feeling of life, as if the glass that had been inverted over me was gone and I was left to float free for the first time.

"This is all there is," we seemed to say together. The boat we sat in was the way in which our mind interpreted the energy that was. The same was true of the water below and the sky above.

We could now experience it all free from the bias of anticipation and expectation, free from ego, and simply be one with the energy that was.

"This is all there is," we said together. "This is everything."

"This is nothing. This is you, this is me, this is us."

This came from the collective voice of the sea.

There was a moment of being overwhelmed with an awareness of my own uniqueness as much as my own connectedness.

My actions were my own. They were so entwined in the actions of existence that I was a part of the whole; an individual so deeply connected. The energy that flowed through and around both fed and was fed by everything in existence. I do not think I have ever felt the same sense of community before or since.

My consciousness moved. It felt like I was a baby kicking in the womb. Not acting out of want or need. Simply withdrawing and expanding as I settled into my Universe. When the Love that flowed through expanded, it did not reduce the Love that flowed out, it added to it. In small, infinitesimal ways the Universe was a part of me, and I it.

My consciousness floated there for a moment, in that gentle push and pull of existence, or was it for an eternity?

Inside. Outside. Within. Without. It was all one. There was a final expression of a thought as I felt my existence transcend. There was a sensation of understanding. There was also a sensation of grounding as a part of me held on and tried to attach feelings to what was, tried to put boundaries to what was boundless.

"I know what it is to be free now," my mind seemed to say as it let go. "This is what it is like to be released from the human experience. We are not what or where. We simply are."

The boundaries between my senses blurred. The borders between earth and sky, between touch and taste, between he and I disappeared. It seemed as if we all came together seamlessly. As if all of existence were one. As if time and space no longer formed linear dimensions. They were what they were, simply markers for what was or would be. Not what is.

"Calm," is what our collective essence seemed to resonate. It shimmered around my own presence. "Content." is what came back.

There is a weightlessness of the spirit when it is a part of something larger. When we are not alone as individuals we are whole. It is not unlike the feeling of being with a group of close friends; not elated or overjoyed, simply content and warmed by the Love that is shared.

The very senses that enabled me to translate this experience into something I could comprehend, limited my ability to fully realize that feeling for what it was. The very walls that once protected me now prevented me from being complete in full awareness.

A rock does not know happiness or unhappiness. It simply knows that it is. An animal understands the happiness of being fed and the pain of the flesh. It recognizes the energy of Love even if it cannot describe the Love it feels in words. A man or woman may understand Love on a small scale but cannot know the enormity of its potential.

Each understands Love and emptiness from a different vantage point without fully realizing that it is only Love that can bring us closer to our own divinity.

Every step we take may seem like an eternity while in it. It is not. It is simply because each step is an experience unto itself, with a limiting lens of understanding.

It is through the spirit that we weave those perspectives together, interlacing the long threads of our experiences into a single tapestry. That tapestry is the source from which our consciousness grows.

As each thread passes in one direction or another, with each warp and woof of the loom, our spirit grows. It becomes more aware with moments of enlightenment. As our awareness grows, our consciousness expands and evolves, our energy overflows our own boundaries to explore new levels of consciousness and being.

It was a moment for me, and in that moment I understood the endless number of worlds and infinite forms through which to explore. I realized there is no sequence in which to explore them. There is no ladder to climb or path to follow. In every direction there is simply a new vantage point to be found from which to view the sea of existence.

Jeff Cannon

Your consciousness is your guide. Your spirit is the conduit through which to experience your journey. Those are the only constants.

Your energy will inhabit countless forms and shapes. With each transformation your consciousness creates a new classroom for the lesson you are to learn. You may spend a millennium as a stone being only aware of the ways in which grains of sand combine and erode to create the pebbles and rocks and boulders that house the energy that is you.

With every classroom you learn the lessons of fear and isolation that can only be known as an unseen bacterium. You may spend entire lives as a human in anger and regret turning away from others and refusing to help or to be helped, until you discover a life as a single person in Love and being Loved.

With every life you learn to stay open, to accept energy from others and to share yours in return. You will learn that growth only occurs when you help those around you to grow. It is in that knowledge that you will truly find the way within yourself.

There is no set path to follow. There are no directions to chart your course by. There are only experiences to explore. Each experience will lead you to the next as you open up to Love and to existence. That is the inevitability of existence. In the end you will be a part of it, but the path to get there is yours to find.

Once a step is taken there is no going back. Within a single life you may learn what it is to be alone. You may learn what it is to lose Love. You may also learn what it is to be a part of someone and something larger than yourself. Each is an infinitely small fraction of what it is to be part of a larger whole.

Within all of this you may not touch the void directly, but you will learn of it. Every time you recoil in pain, you learn what it is like to reconnect with the Love that is all around. When you do not fit comfortably with another, when you feel as if you are alone, you learn what it means to be awash in Love all over again.

It is as if you forever turn the piece that is you this way and that until you find a way to fit perfectly into the puzzle that is existence. With each twist and turn you grow aware of how it feels to be in perfect balance and harmony.

Every lifetime helps you to burnish the edges of your existence until we all fit within the perfection that is Love. Each experience you take brings us all one step closer to completing our tapestry together.

In the end, we find ourselves and realize that we are precisely where we have always known we should be. Beautiful and perfect with all of our imperfections intact; calm and content with who we collectively are.

Without the ocean around us, there was no image of flowing water and waves to fall back on. I closed my eyes and lay back into myself. I felt my own embrace. I had returned.

All around me I watched an intricate dance where the infinite dimensions moved and revolved around each other. Just like an electron spinning around an atom, 3ach dimension was less a fixed plane as it was a series of probabilities. Each plane reflected an emotion, a sense, a taste between which the ebb and flow of energy ran connecting them all through our consciousness.

"How long can we stay here?" It was the echo of my own thoughts coming through. I knew my own answer.

"How long have we spent here?"

"There is no time. There is only this." I echoed to me.

I was again released, floating and able to see time, not as a linear plane, but as yet another dimension. Time ceased being a marker for me. It is just like smell or taste or longitude or latitude, it is simply another way to describe the energy of an event; a way I no longer needed in the here and now.

That night it came as a slow roll. Almost as a wave. I felt whatever connection I had was broken. There was a flash of, of all things, of a walrus colony basking in the sun on a rocky point. It was as if one walrus rolled over, which caused every other walrus to shuffle in response. I less moved, as much as I was moved.

"Where did that come from?" I thought. And the moment I did I wished I had not. I realized in the smallest fraction of a nanosecond that what my friend had said so many eons ago was true. Once you send a thought out you cannot take it back.

If I had arms I would have flailed them in an attempt to grab onto that wisp of an idea. I knew that I could not. Instead I relaxed and smiled to myself feeling the nothingness that was around me. I could feel it and sense it, but I could not hold it. There was no tiller; there was no boat, there was no ocean. There was no me. There simply was.

Jeff Cannon

That moment lasted an eternity. I was, once again, aware of the greater presence of Love. It spoke to me without sound or feeling. It spoke in the true voice of existence.

I understood. It was time.

MY AWAKENING

I remember at some point the feeling, not of lightness but of weight. It was the weight of my body being returned to me. It felt like I was following a rope that led down into the water. It was not unlike the feeling of following an anchor chain down to the seabed or that wonderful feeling in meditation when you become aware of following your mind to a point of emptiness. It is not uncomfortable, but it is a realization.

With each handhold I pulled myself further into the physical world. I felt the solidity of my body form around me. I felt the softness of the bed. I felt the coolness of the air and began to be aware of the sounds of the island.

It was not an uncomfortable passage. It was what I had expected would happen. It was what I knew had to be.

I slept the rest of that night without dreaming. Instead, I reacquainted myself with my world and with my very human self. I embraced my senses as well as my lack of senses until the sun welcomed me back to life.

I was at peace like I never have been, I simply floated in bed, knowing that I no longer had to sail, for I was that point on the horizon where the sea meets the stars.

FINAL DAY

That final day for us on Ithaca was the same as the final day on any vacation. It was a happy sadness in which we all knew we had been a part of something truly special. There were bags to carry down and load into our familiar jeep, the one we once laughed at but would now miss.

There were goodbyes to say. But there was also the joy in knowing that we had all been a part of something very, very special. It was that wonderful feeling of the Love we all shared during our time together.

Our travel was the reverse of the trip that brought us to Ithaca. Every step moved further and further away from the slow-moving balance we had found. From ferry to taxi to small plane to London and then New York, we were re-engaged with the modern world of mobile phones and news updates.

By the time we arrived back in the states, I cannot say our transformation to the 21st Century was complete. That would take much longer, if it ever arrived. To this day I am not sure it has. But I'm okay with that.

For me, it was not just a vacation. It was a conversation that continues on to this day. I still see my friend from time to time.

He appears mostly while coming out of surgeries, in that twilight hour when I am not sure if I am conscious or unconscious.

Our conversations continue, but each is a distant echo of that first experience we shared, floating in the sea above Ithaca, that remains the most memorable.

POST SCRIPT - THE HUMAN EXPERIENCE

I am forever reminded that the human experience is just that, an experience. It is a series of lessons to be explored and learned from. Each helps us to grow and evolve on our own terms and as a part of the greater whole. Each prepares us for the infinite nature of Love that we will ultimately discover is right here within us. It always has been, it always will be.

Regardless of the path we take our spirit grows until we eventually find the Love we seek within ourselves. Each of us inevitably arrives at our destination. That is the point where we become aware of the true energy of Love, and we learn that Love comes freely once we learn to give our Love freely and without want of anything in return.

Only when you find the Love that is within you can you discover the true nature of Love that can be had with another. Love is the beauty of the soul. Once you learn to embrace it and share it can you allow it in. The moment you allow Love in, it will forever be there so that it flows through you and empowers you.

POST SCRIPT - YOUR JOURNEY

In truth your journey is not long. The Human Experience is actually rather short. It is truly understood at only two points along the way. The first is the moment before birth. The second is the moment after passing. Everything else is confusion broken by moments of enlightenment. That confusion is caused by the duality you feel between the physical and the metaphysical, the human and the divine that is within you.

The confusion you feel is what provides you the choice from which to find your path. Remember, it is the journey that matters, not the destination. This is something we are all aware of as we explore our existence and as we travel through the human experience.

When you are born you learn to live in the physical body you have found yourself in. When you emerge from the womb you are taught to breathe with a spank. From that that point on you begin to rely on others for your physical needs, for food and care and protection.

As you adapt to the world around you, you become aware of the capabilities and limitations of your physical self. The more aware you become of your minds and body, the more aware you become of its limitations and how much your mind and body isolates your spirit from those around you.

Through your loneliness you are reminded of your spirit. You are reminded of your higher needs. You learn that you can move through the boundaries that exist with Love, until you can connect with your true self on a spiritual level.

This is why infants Love so freely. They do not know fear or anger. Those emotions are only learned once they are taught how much the physical world separates them from the Love that is all around.

When one becomes aware of the isolation of the body, that is the moment when you truly begin your journey. The rest is a search for the Love that we all know is out there but cannot always reach. That Love is your connection home.

As each of us searches for Love we connect with those around us. We learn how to live with others. We grow aware of the distractions that can keep us from our own transcendence.

We may be distracted by the goals of the physical world. We may even forget what it was that we wanted in the first place.

For some these distraction never exists. For others, they exist all too profoundly. That is partly what guides us on our various paths toward enlightenment and our inevitable transcendence.

Regardless of the path you choose, at some point your spirit guides you to seek the Love you thought you had lost. It is that thought, that you have lost the Love you once had, that drives you to reach out to others. It is only with time that you learn the Love you seek is not found in others, but within yourself. Only when can you grow by connecting to the Love that is all around.

None of these paths is wrong. Each eventually leads to the Love that is. It is all part of the human experience, no matter how many iterations it may take.

Floating in existence as I was, I realized that I could reach further into myself than I ever thought possible because I knew I had no end. I was connected at every point to every point of consciousness in existence. In that, I realized there is no distance. There is no isolation. There is only connection.

You must simply look for it.

POSTSCRIPT - YOUR LIFE MARKERS

I am aware that time and physical space are very human concepts. We use them to measure our experiences. They help us locate an event that we think is lost to existence. I am also aware that with them our ability to transcend the very human world, the ability to understand our endless experience, is locked.

A map limits as much as it helps depending on the vantage point from which it was drawn. It is no different with birth or death. Each is a way for us to begin and end our journey so that we can make sense of the human experience we have found ourselves in. They give each of us a start and a finish to measure our race.

In the end it is not the markers that matter. If you are to find yourself you must reach out and touch the energy that lies behind those markers instead. You must take risks if you are to touch Love freely and without condition. You must remain open to the Love that is given and asked of you.

Even Love that only lasts a moment is important, for it is a channel through which your experience will evolve. The thoughts behind your actions are what create the currents upon which you ride. But it is the actions that are the signposts which will guide you to your thoughts.

The way may not always be easy, but know that the truth is always there. One must do more than simply fall in and out of Love to experience the purity of Love.

To know Love is to pause and reflect. It is to understand the nuances of the infinite as well as those of the mind and body. True Love is found in the trust and faith that is shared. If Love is to thrive and become a part of you rather than just survive within you there is a level of acceptance and understanding if you are to embrace your own frailties. And that is an essential part of understanding the nature of your true self.

There is a forgiveness that must be embraced if your Love is to feed your spirit and the spirits of others. Each frailty is a point of connection that crosses time and space. Each frailty matters.

In many ways your weaknesses and frailties are no different than your emotions. They are more real than longitude and latitude ever will be. They are the winds and the waves and the currents through which you ultimately navigate.

Most will not see them that way. They are blinded by their own minds and bodies. But your frailties are the guideposts in your life, more so than any map will ever be. They are not rules to live by. They are not paths to follow. They are the signposts that tell you there is a choice to be made. That choice will guide you to your next experience, and will show you the way.

When you learn to recognize your weaknesses and emotions for what they are, they ceases to lead and begins to guide. When you learn to see each emotion, you will find they are, in reality, a small window into the dimensions that dance around you, every feeling becomes a path upon which to step toward the Love of existence.

When you learn to ask yourself, 'where am I in my Love?", 'Where am I in my compassion?', 'Am I lost in hate and anger?', 'Will I find myself in understanding?', that is when you will begin to find yourself right where you are.

The emotions and frailties you may dislike in yourself is more real than the locators you commonly use. They are more important than time or East and West, North and South. They show you where your spirit, and where your energy is. Those are the answers that will tell us where you truly are in the sea of existence.

Jeff Cannon

www.ingramcontent.com/pod-product-compliance
Lightning Source LLC.
Chambersburg PA
CBHW071319090426
42738CB00012B/2732